Adult Coloring Book
Patterns for Stress Relieving

Linn Littlebelle

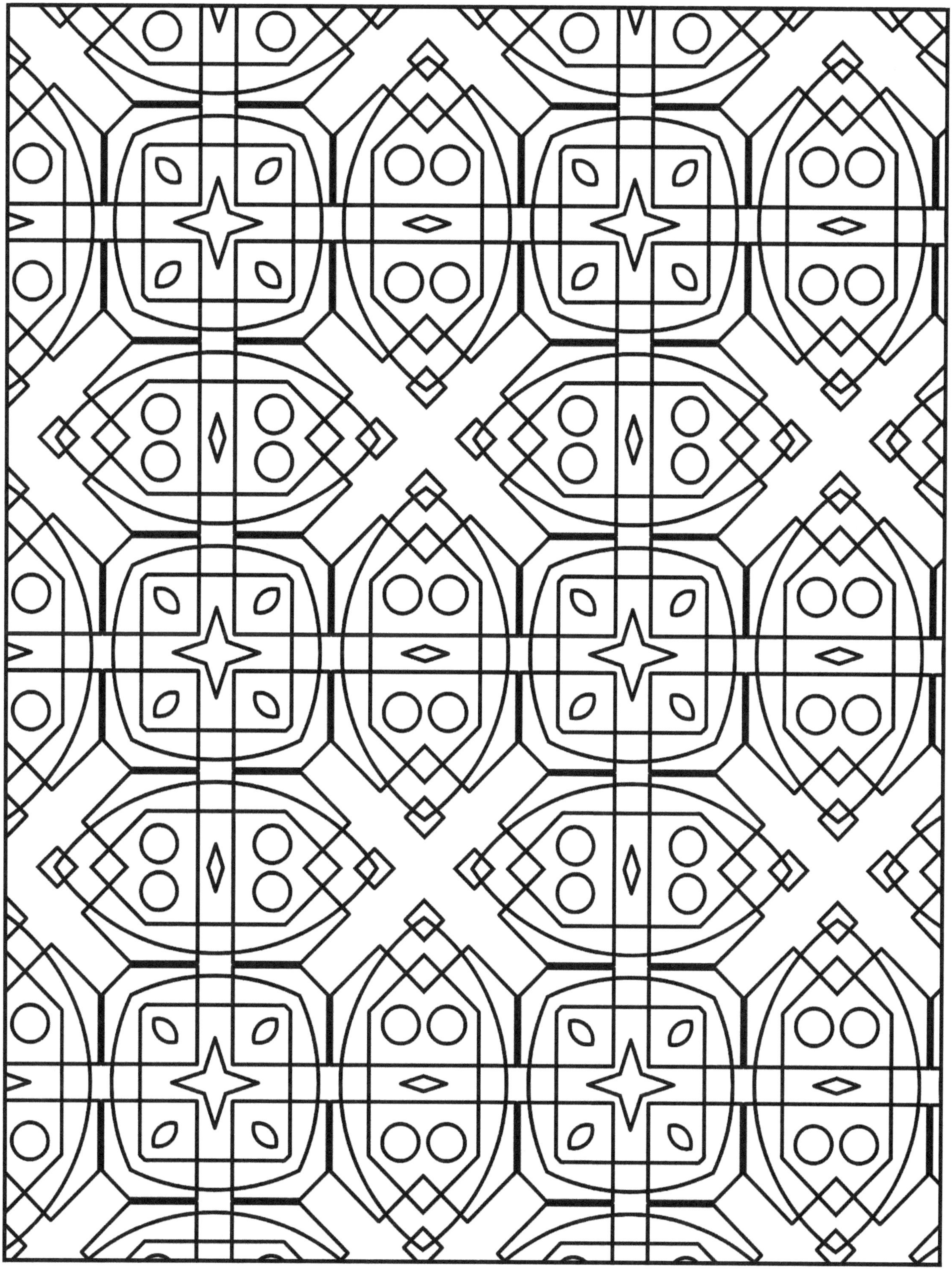

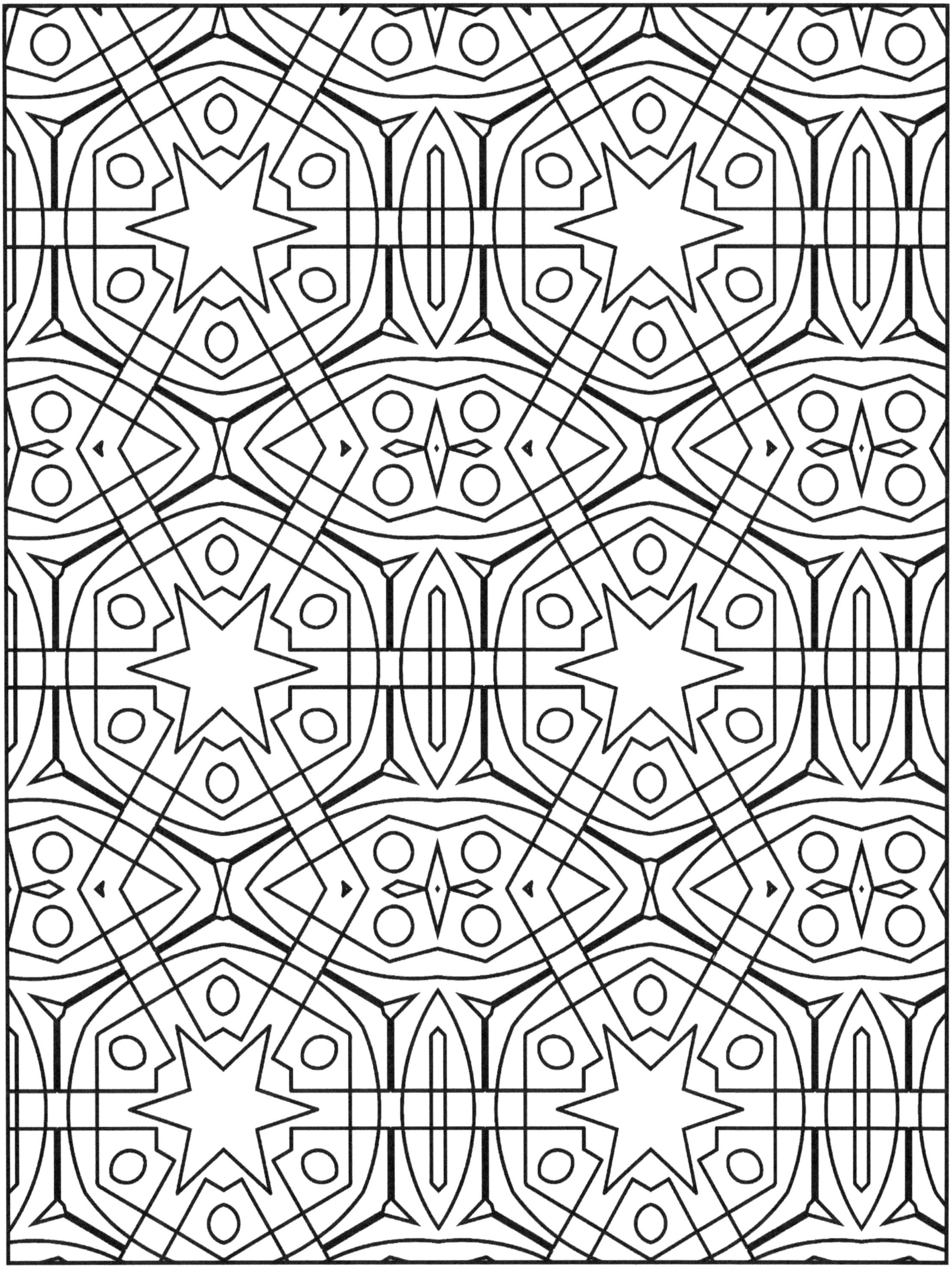

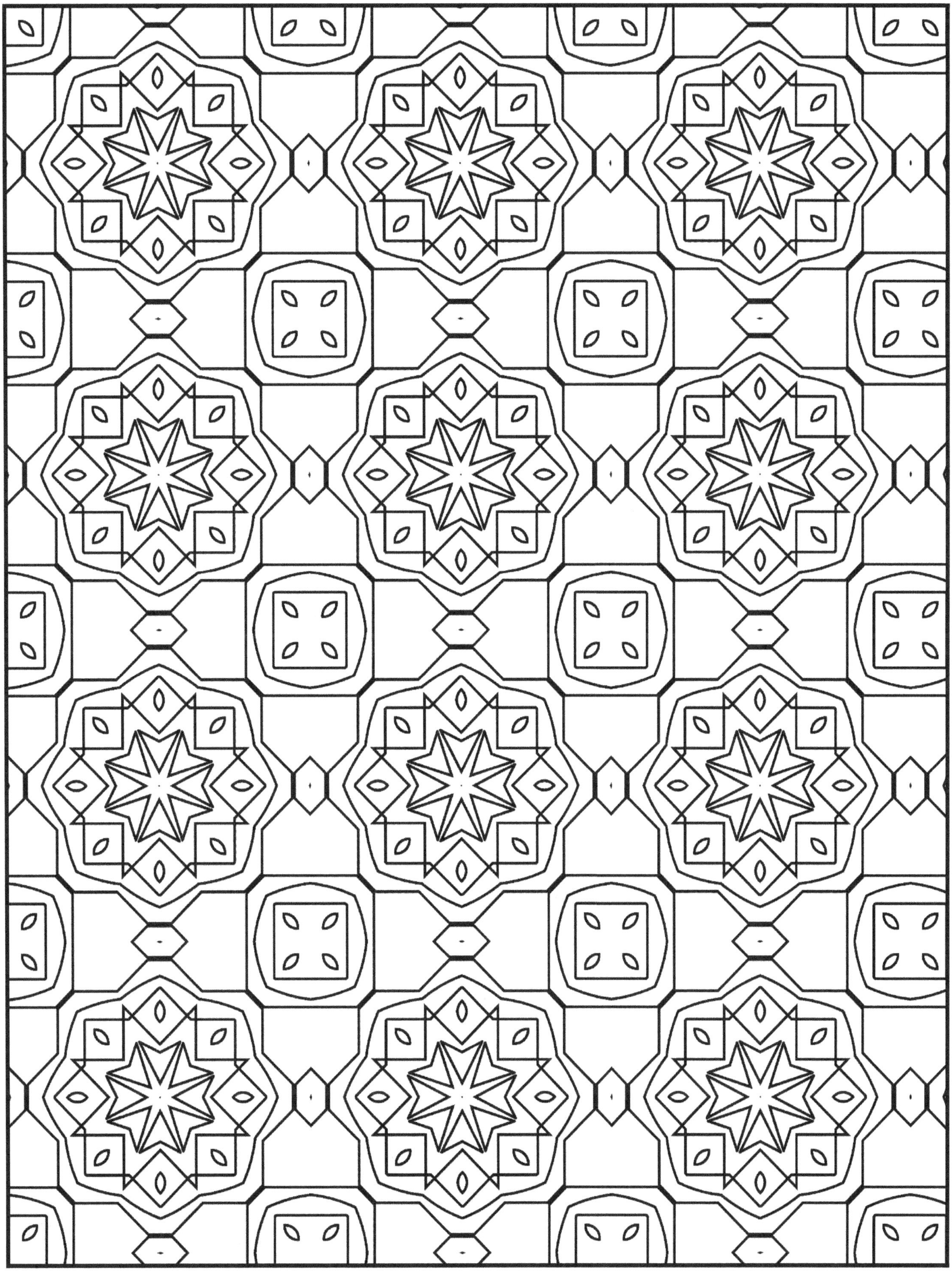

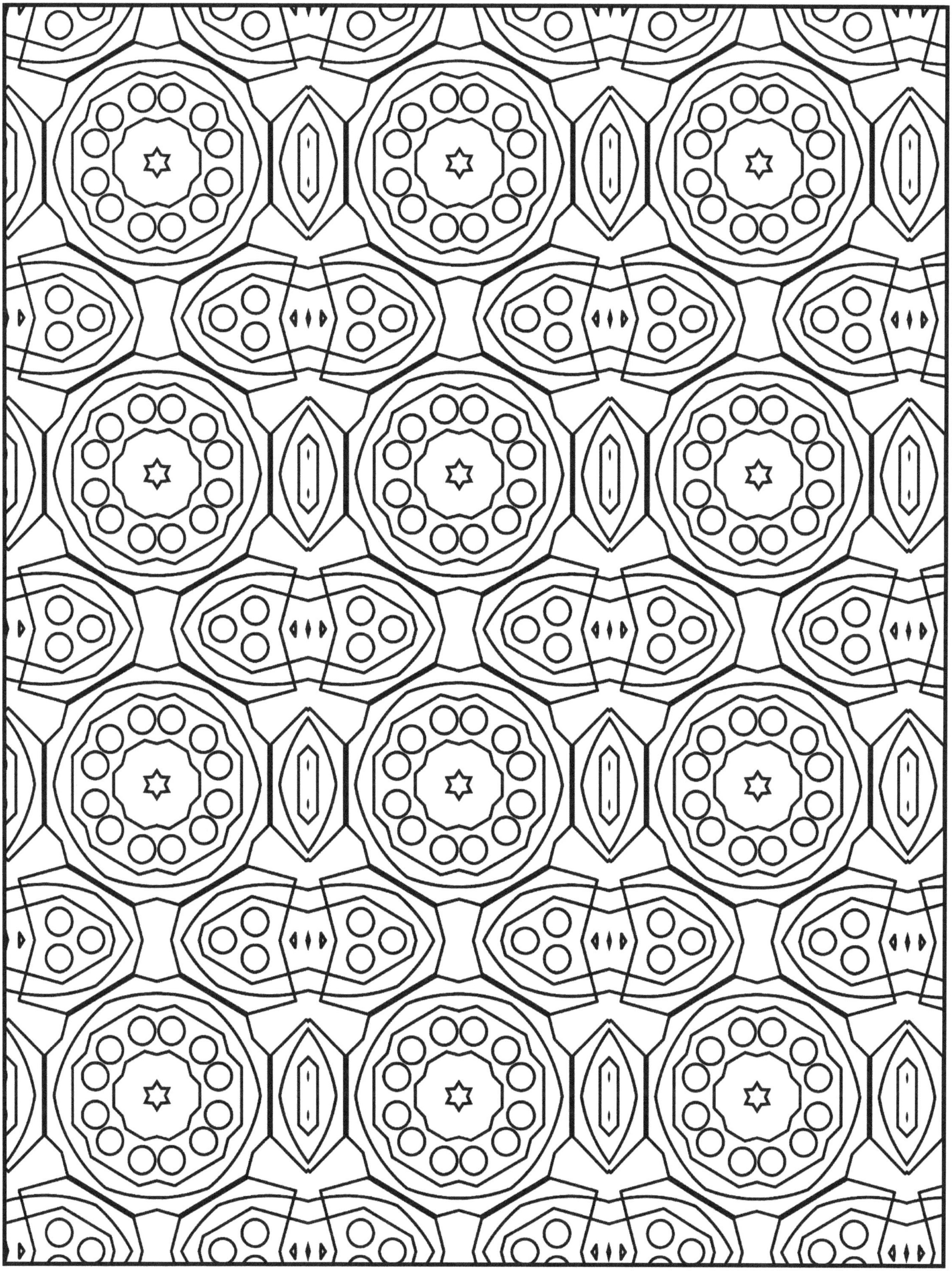

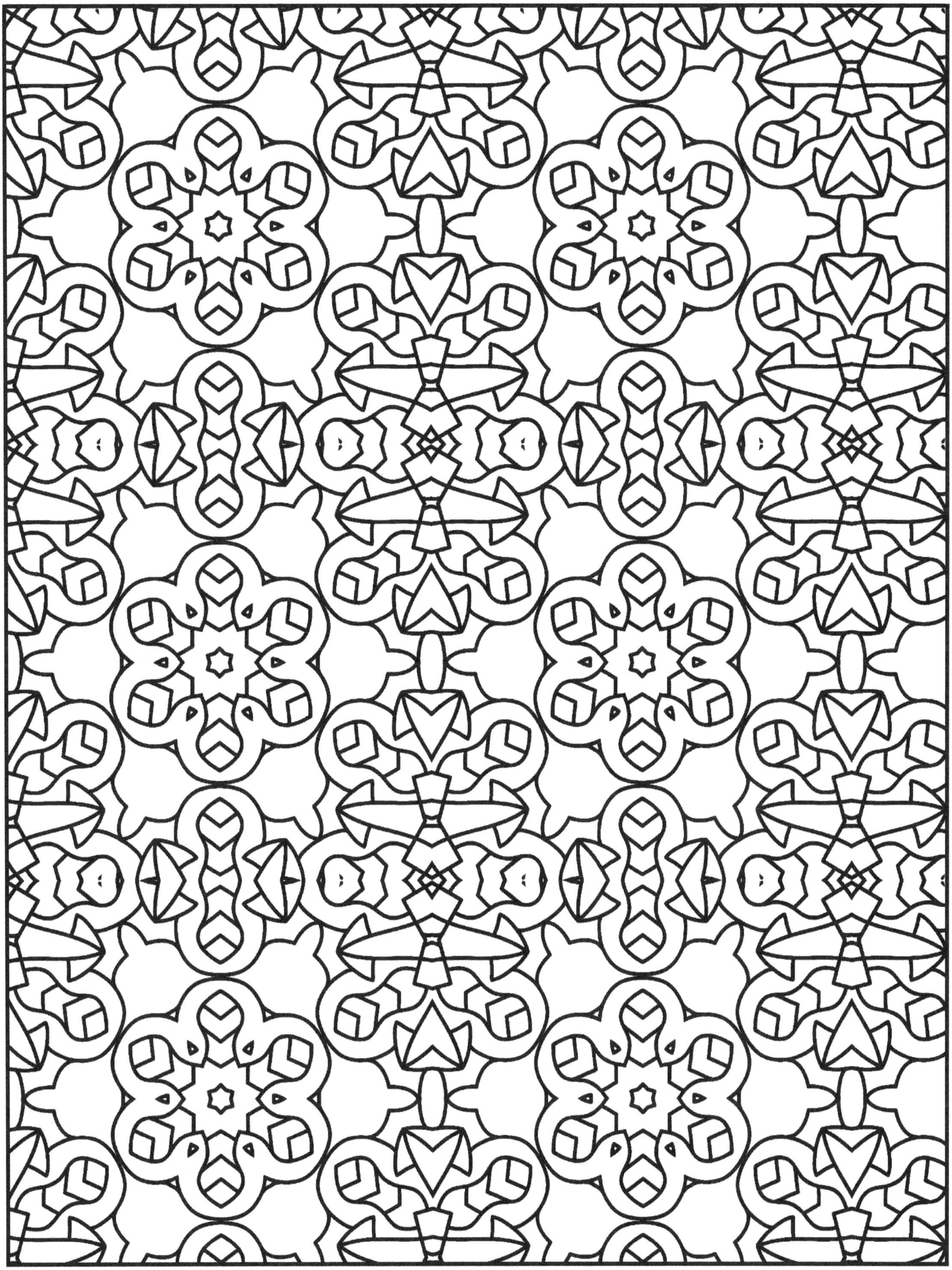

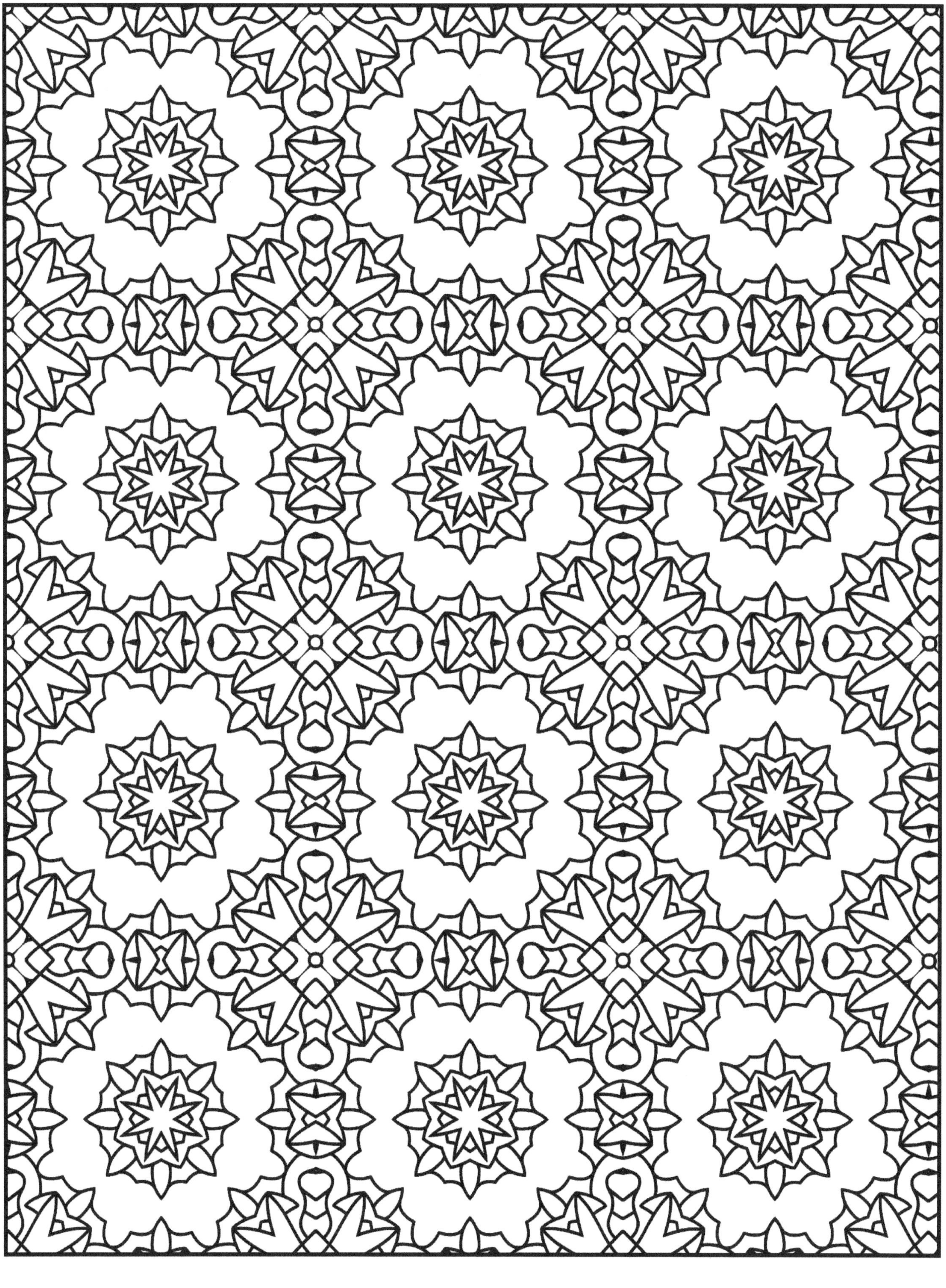

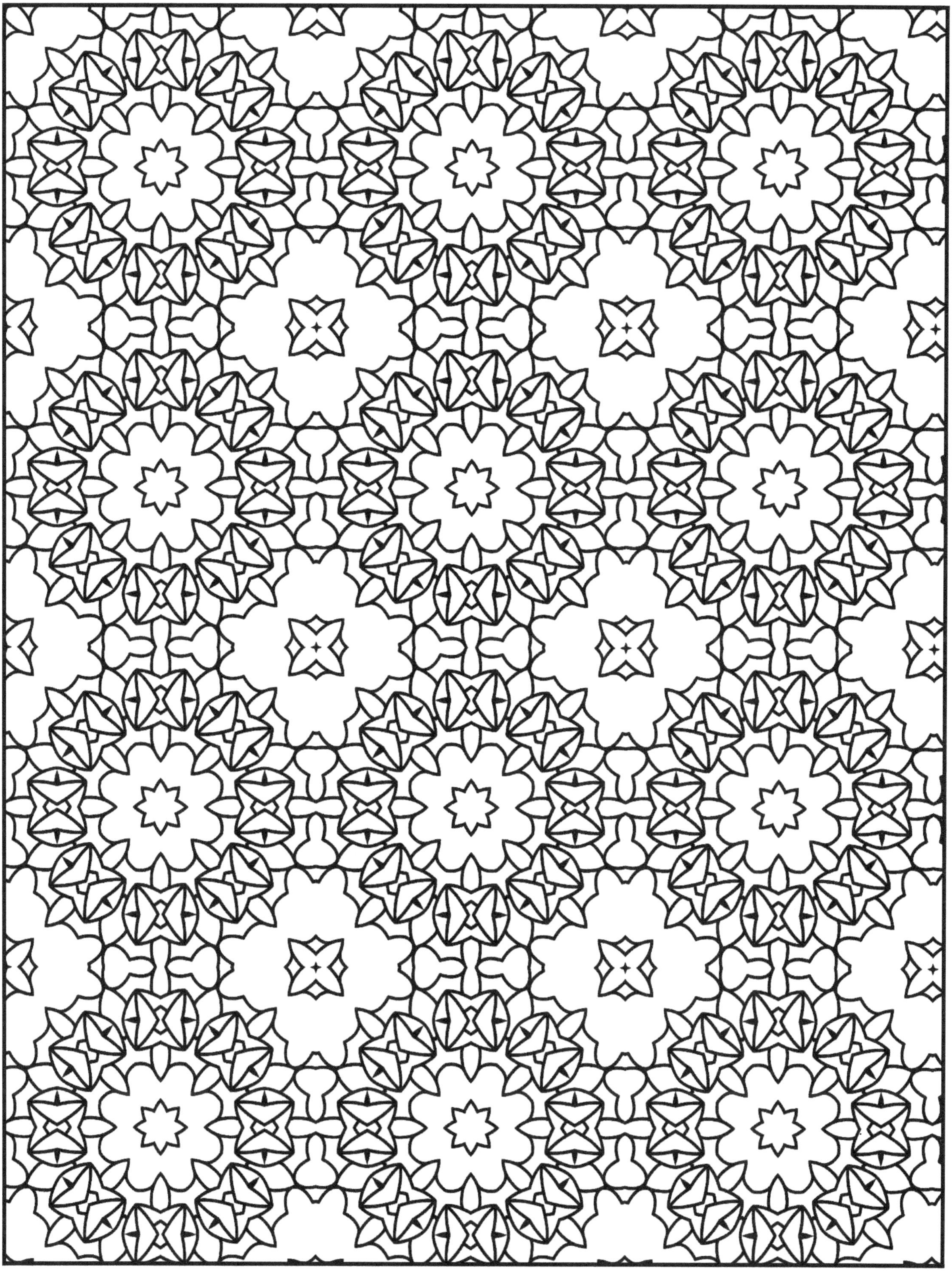

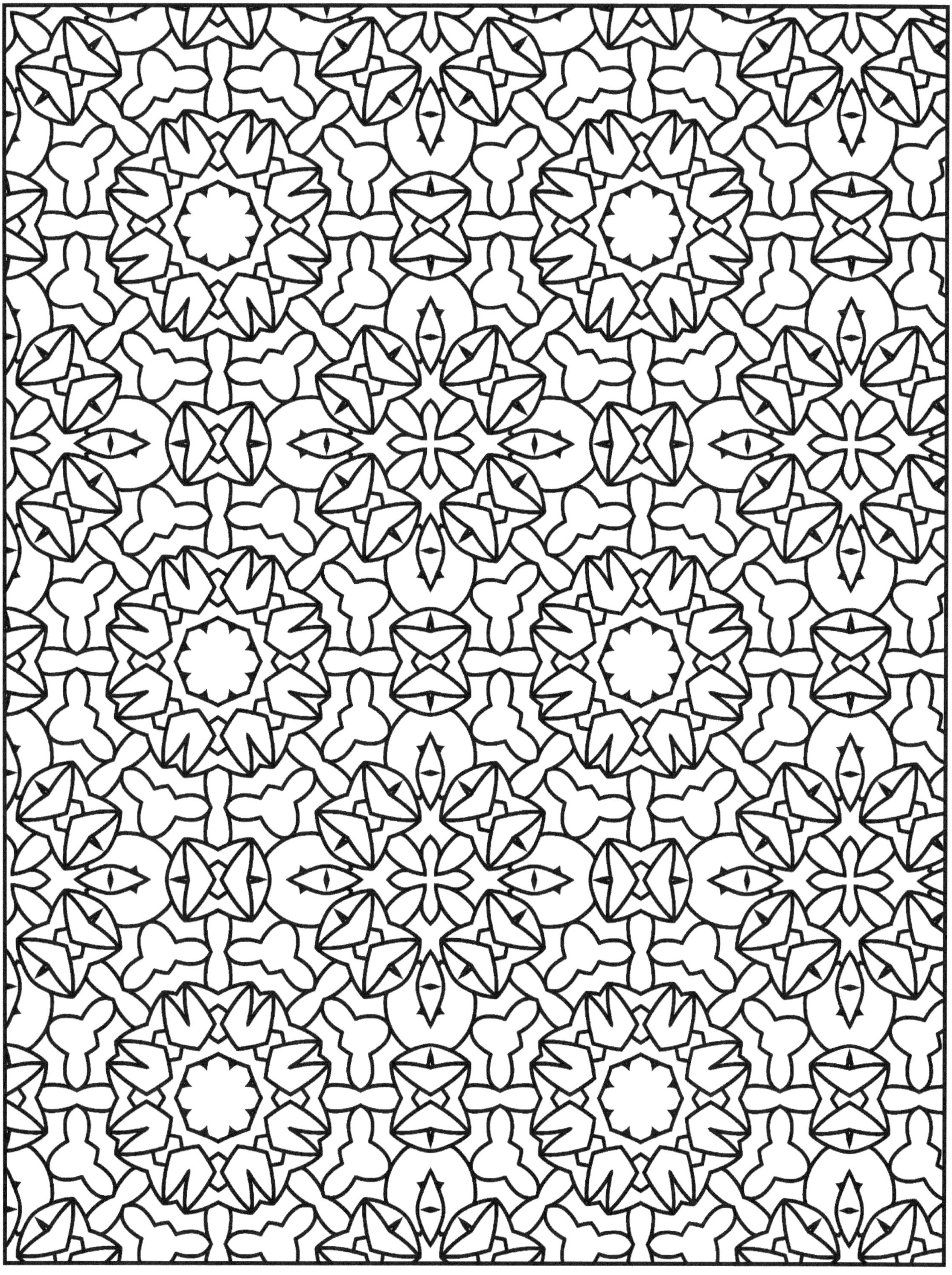

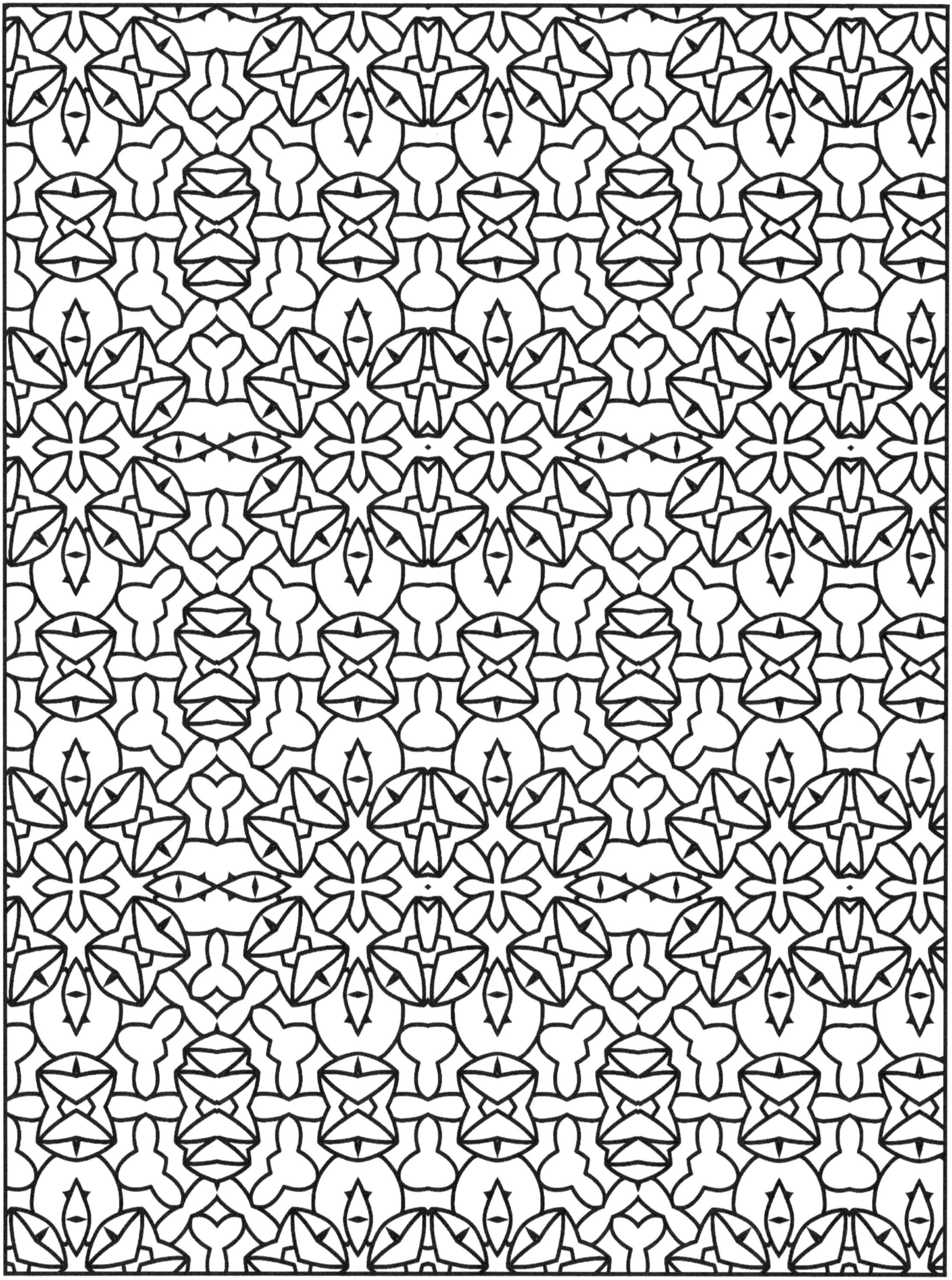

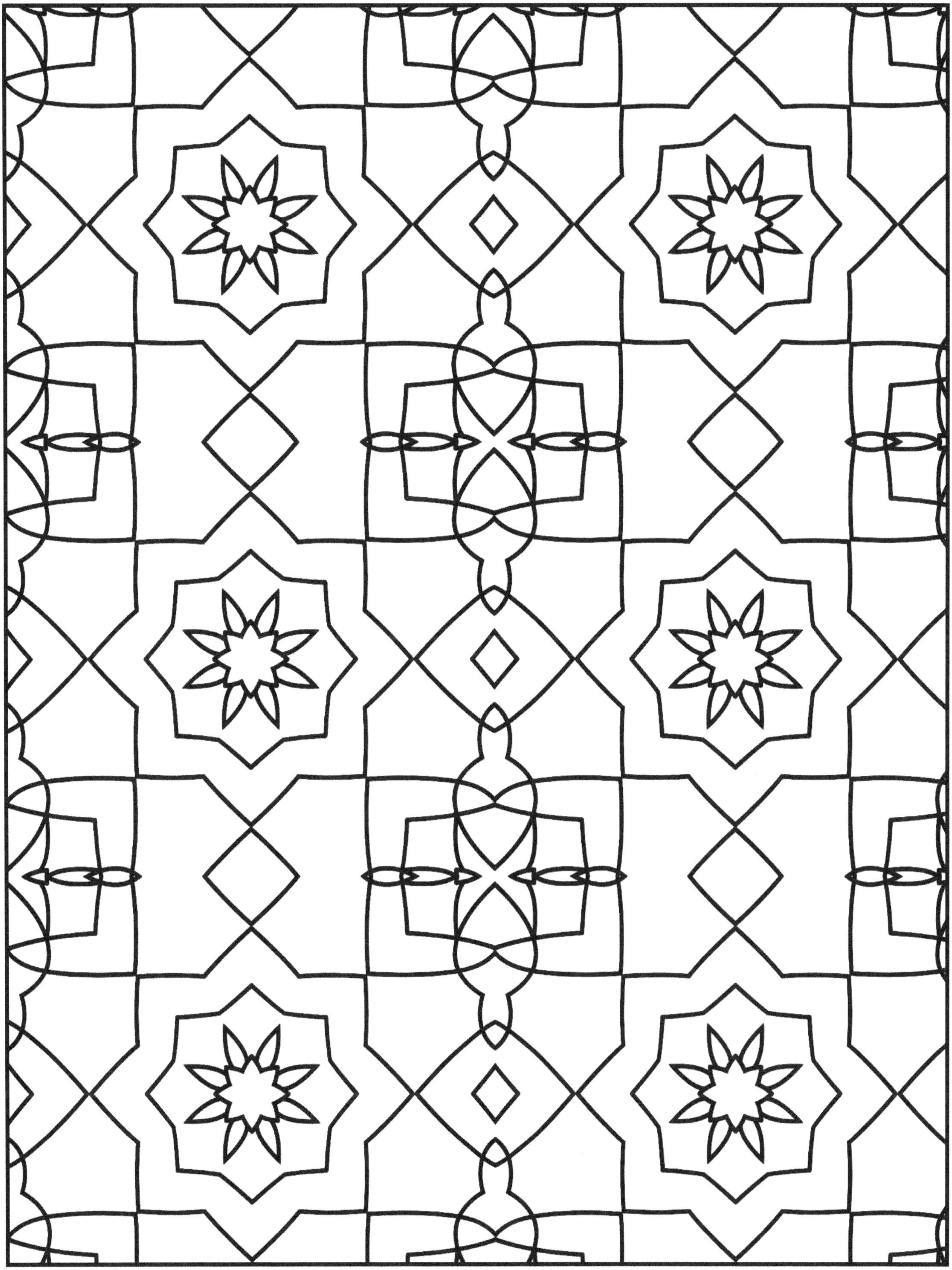

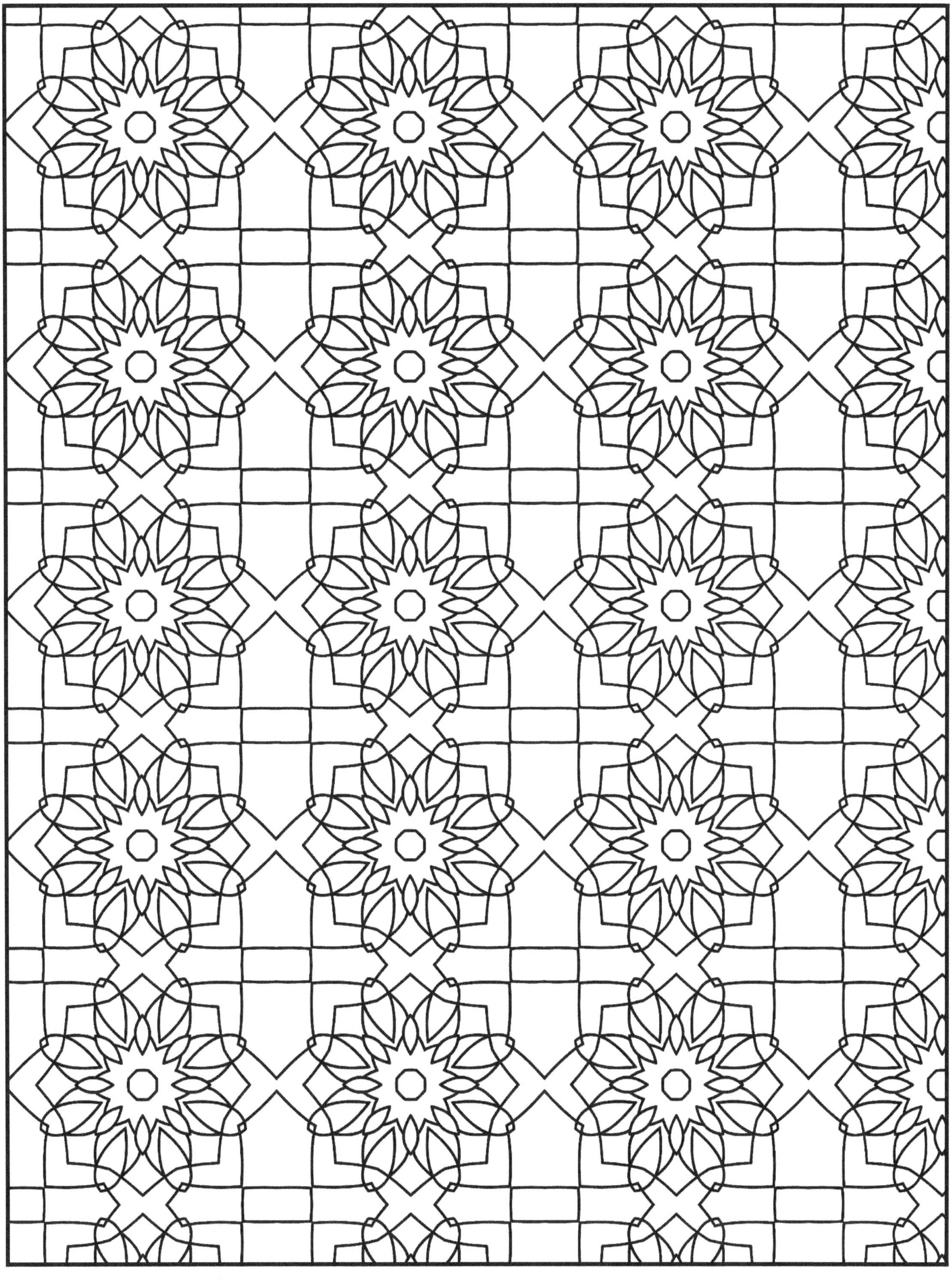

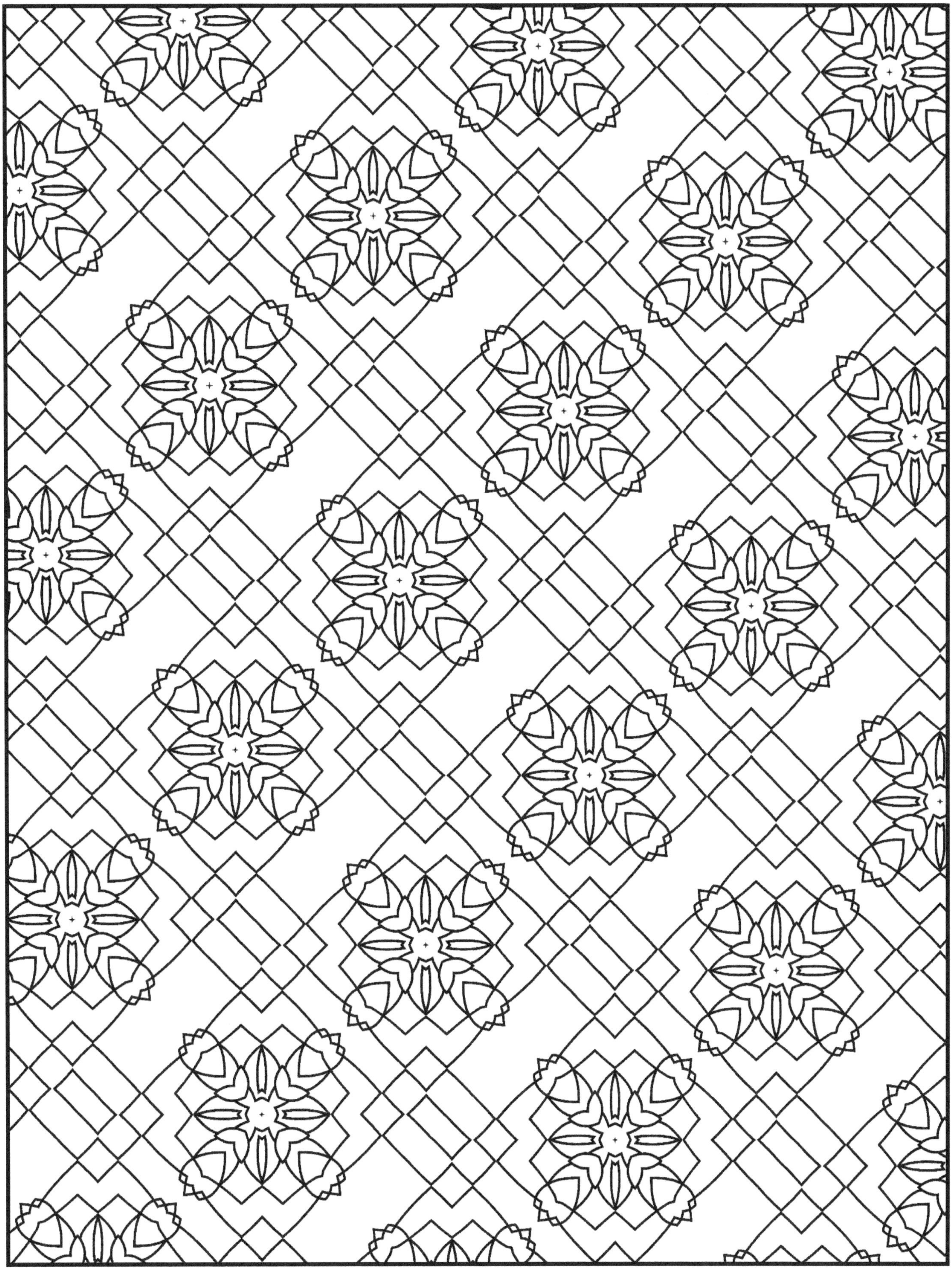

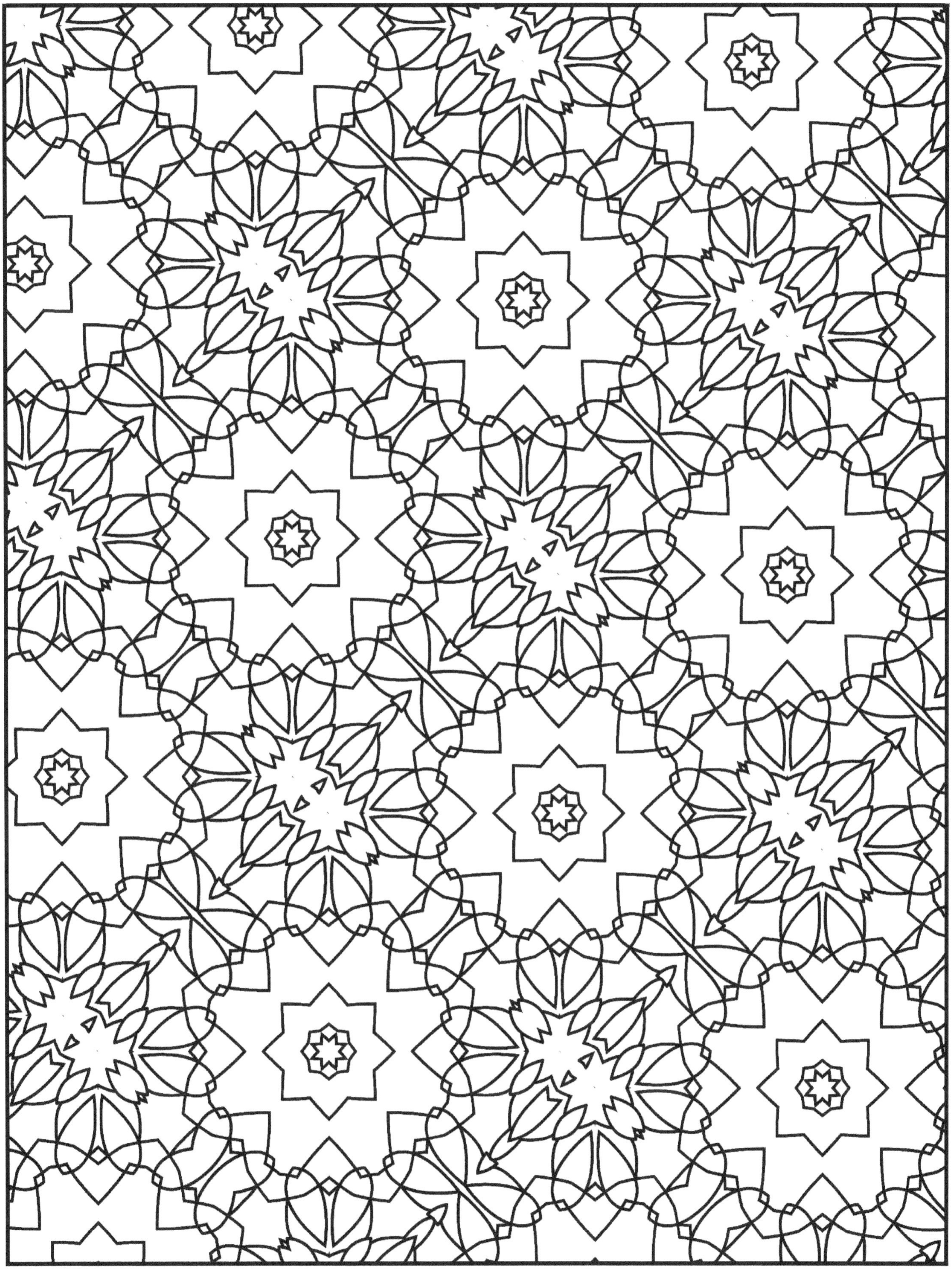

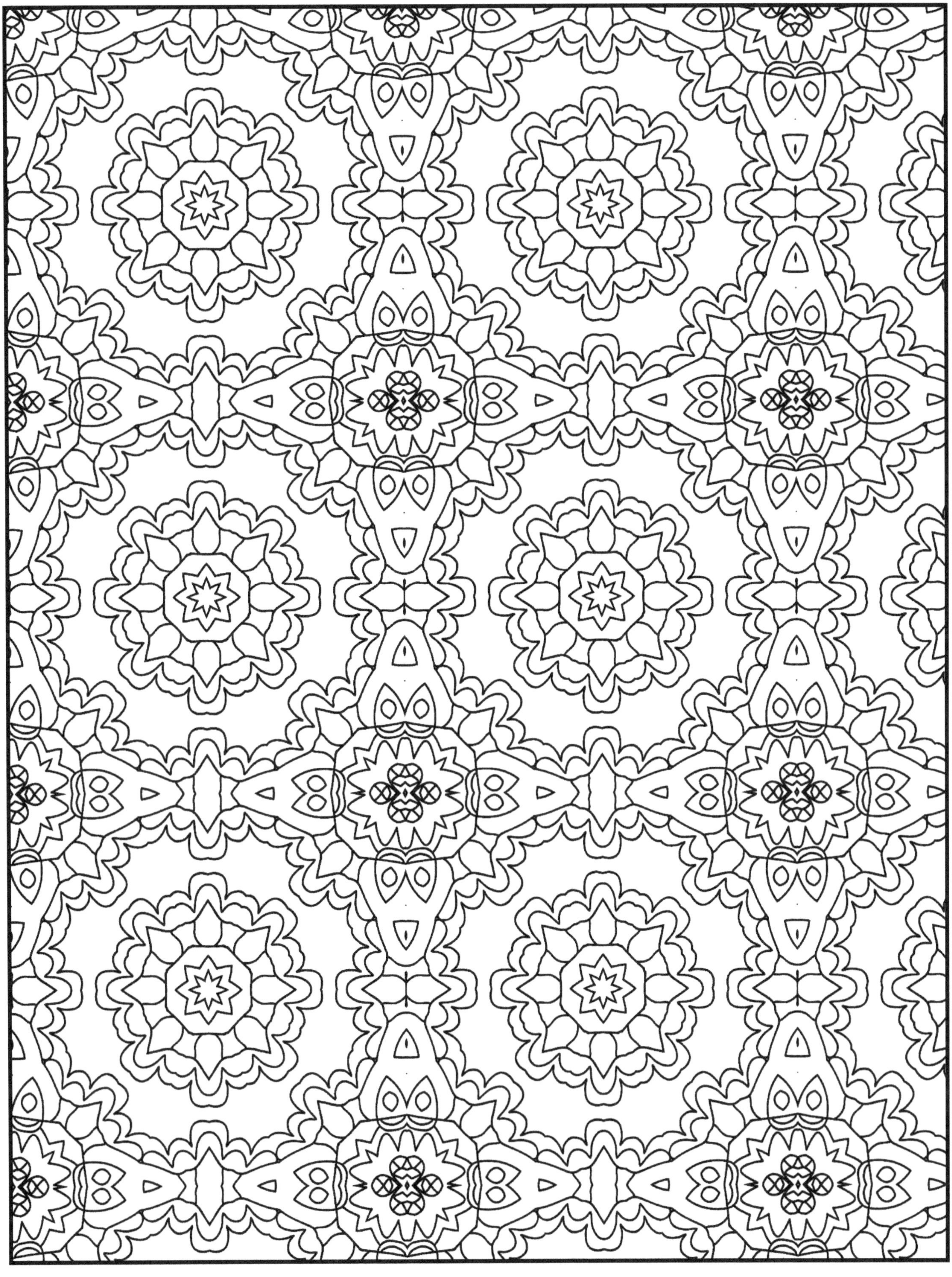

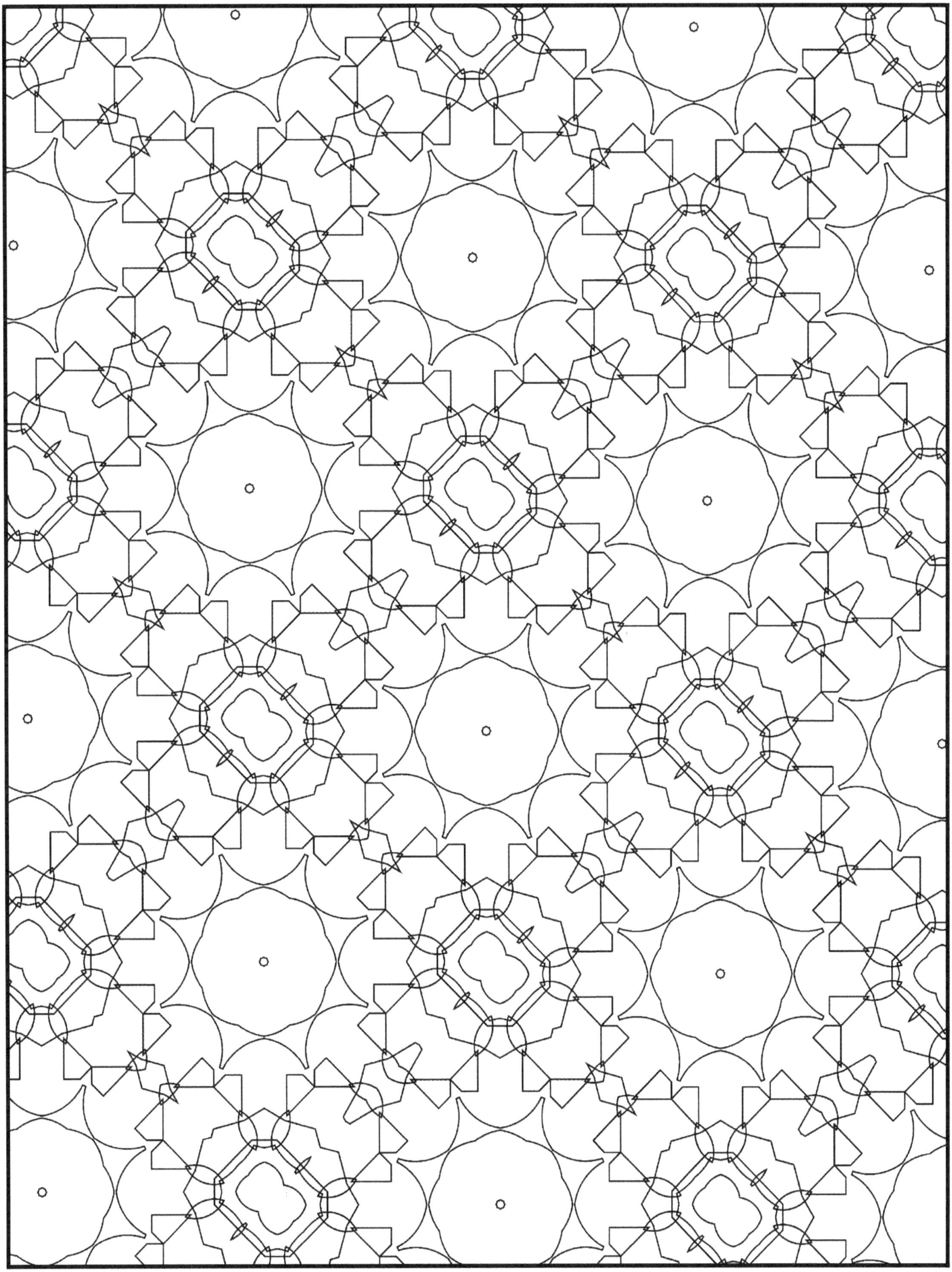

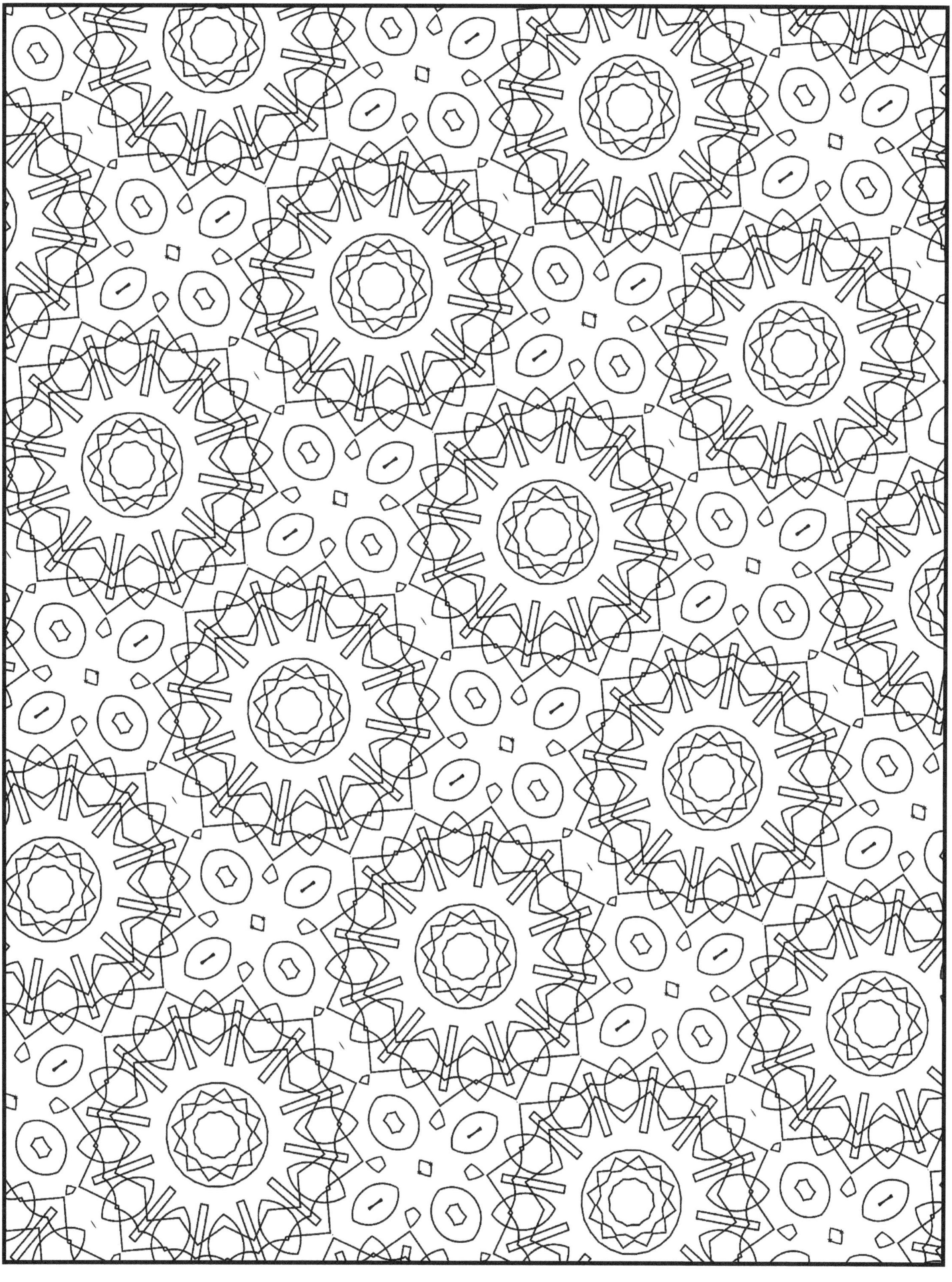

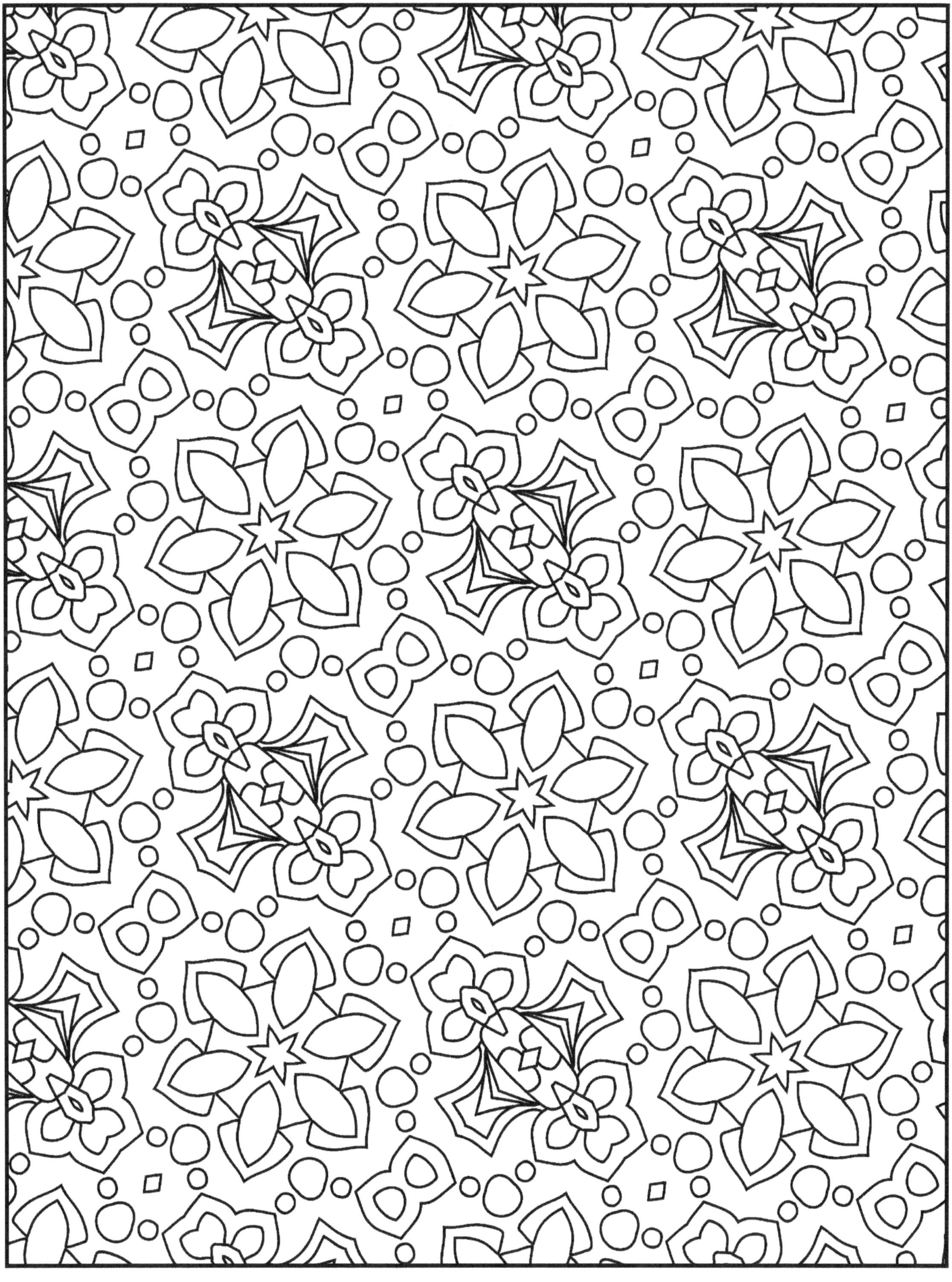

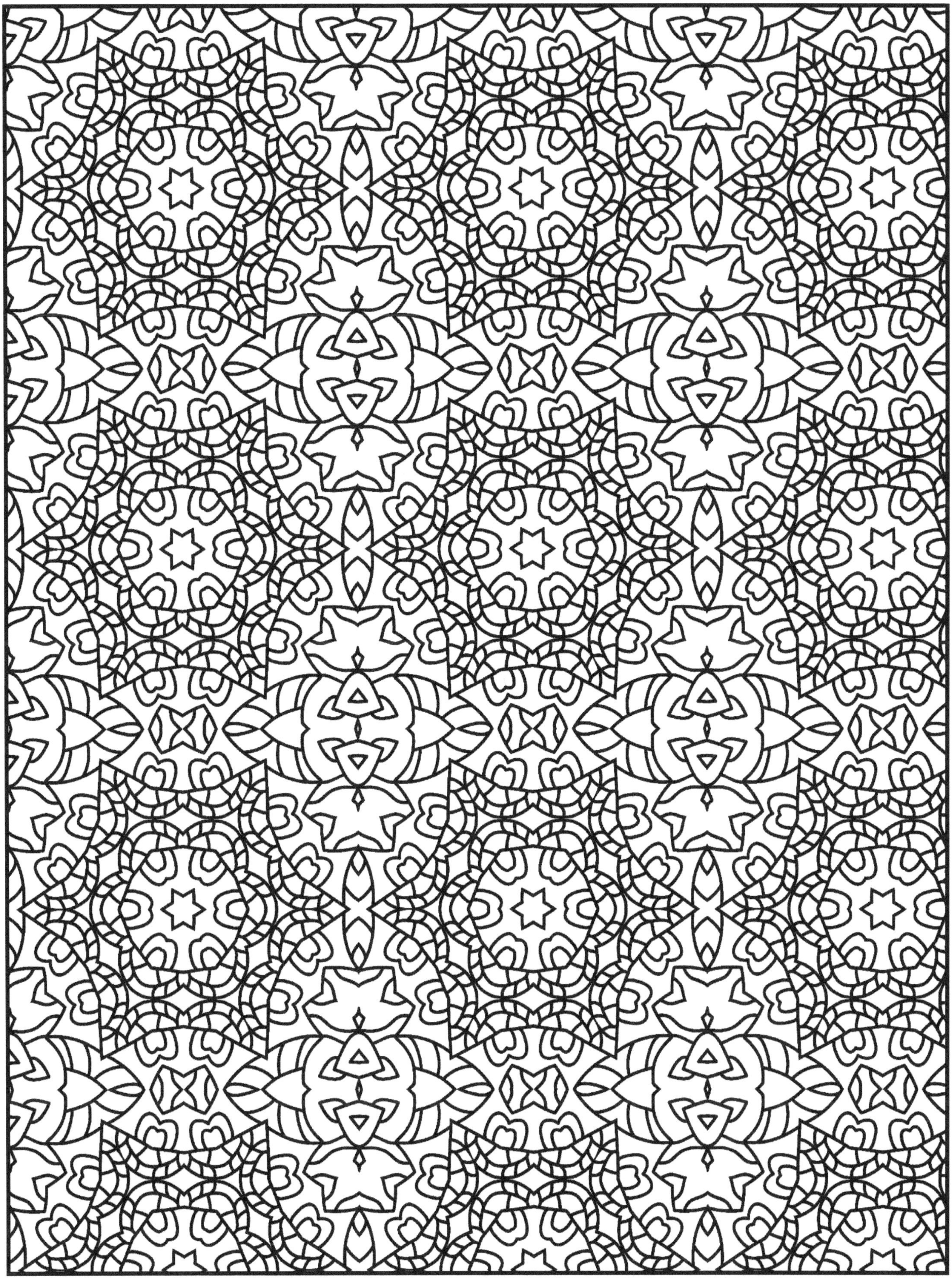

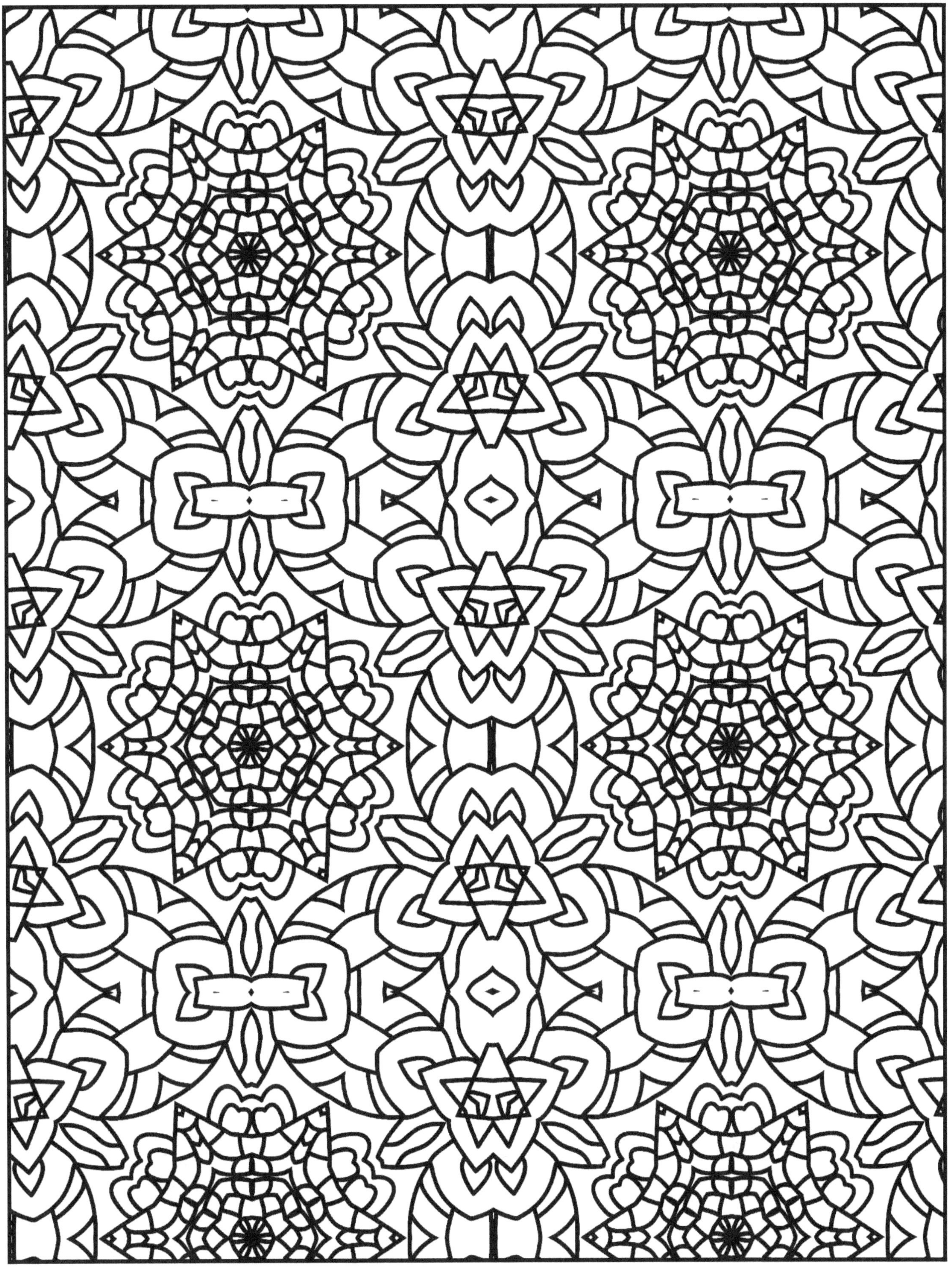

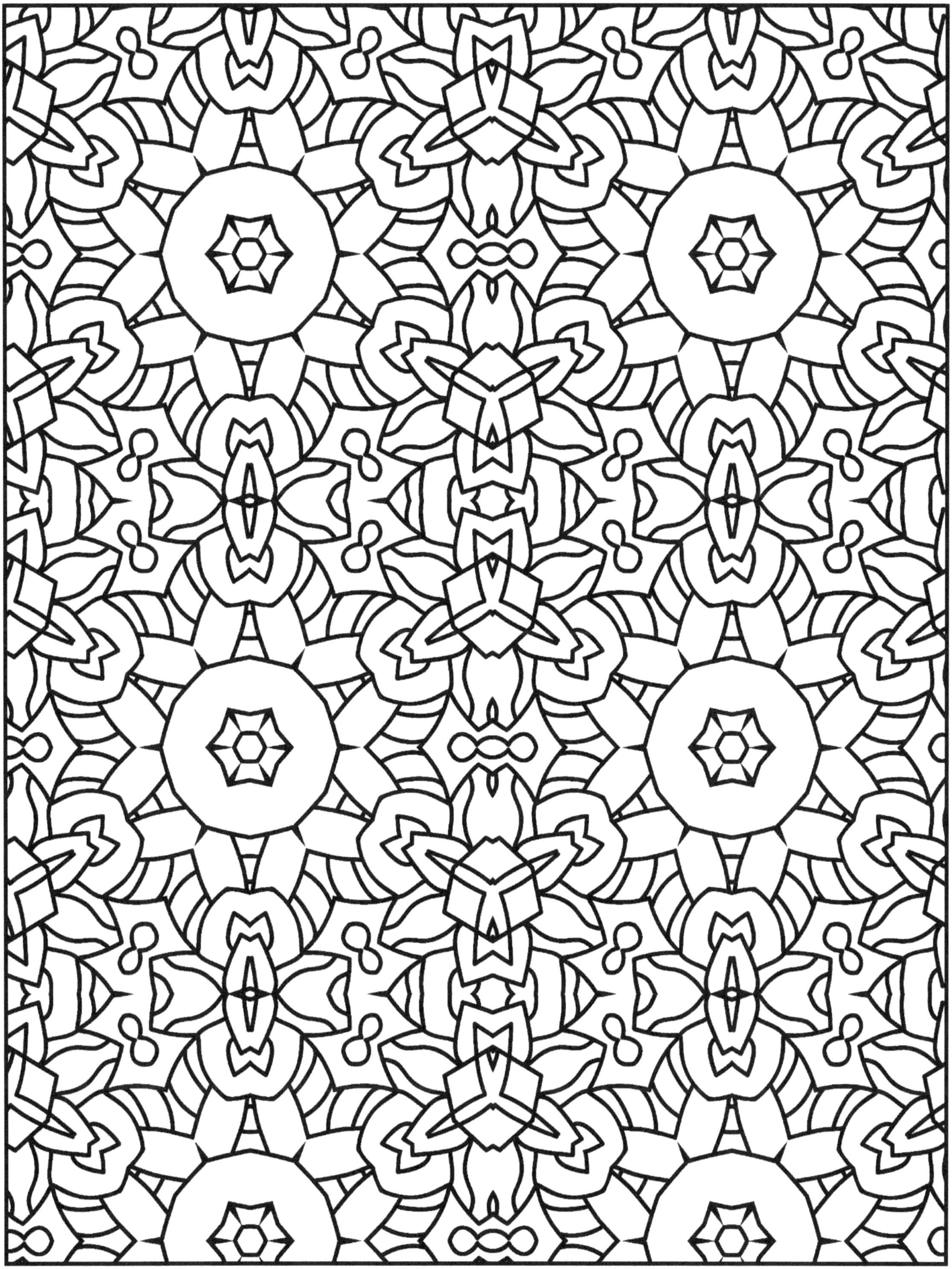

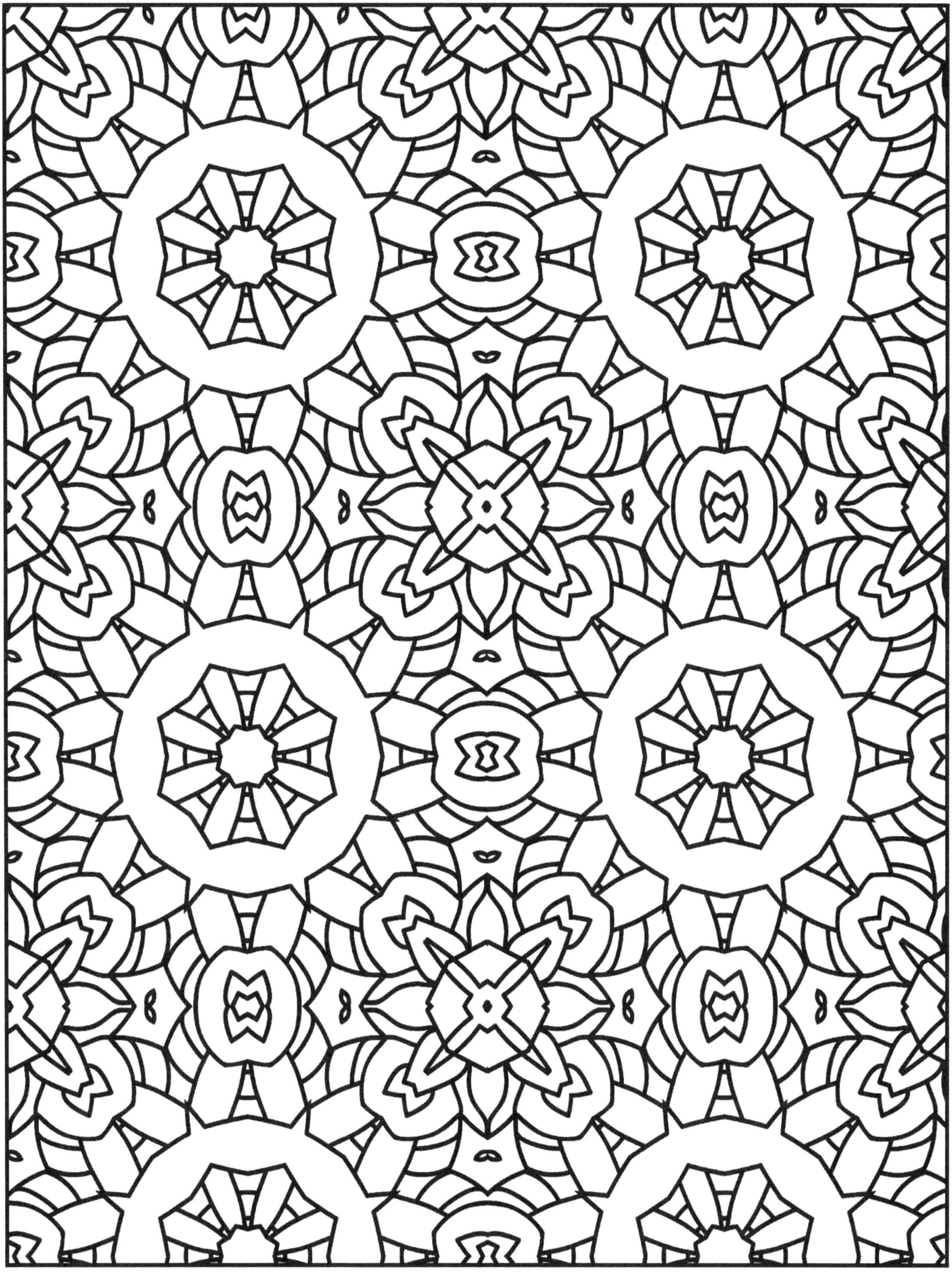

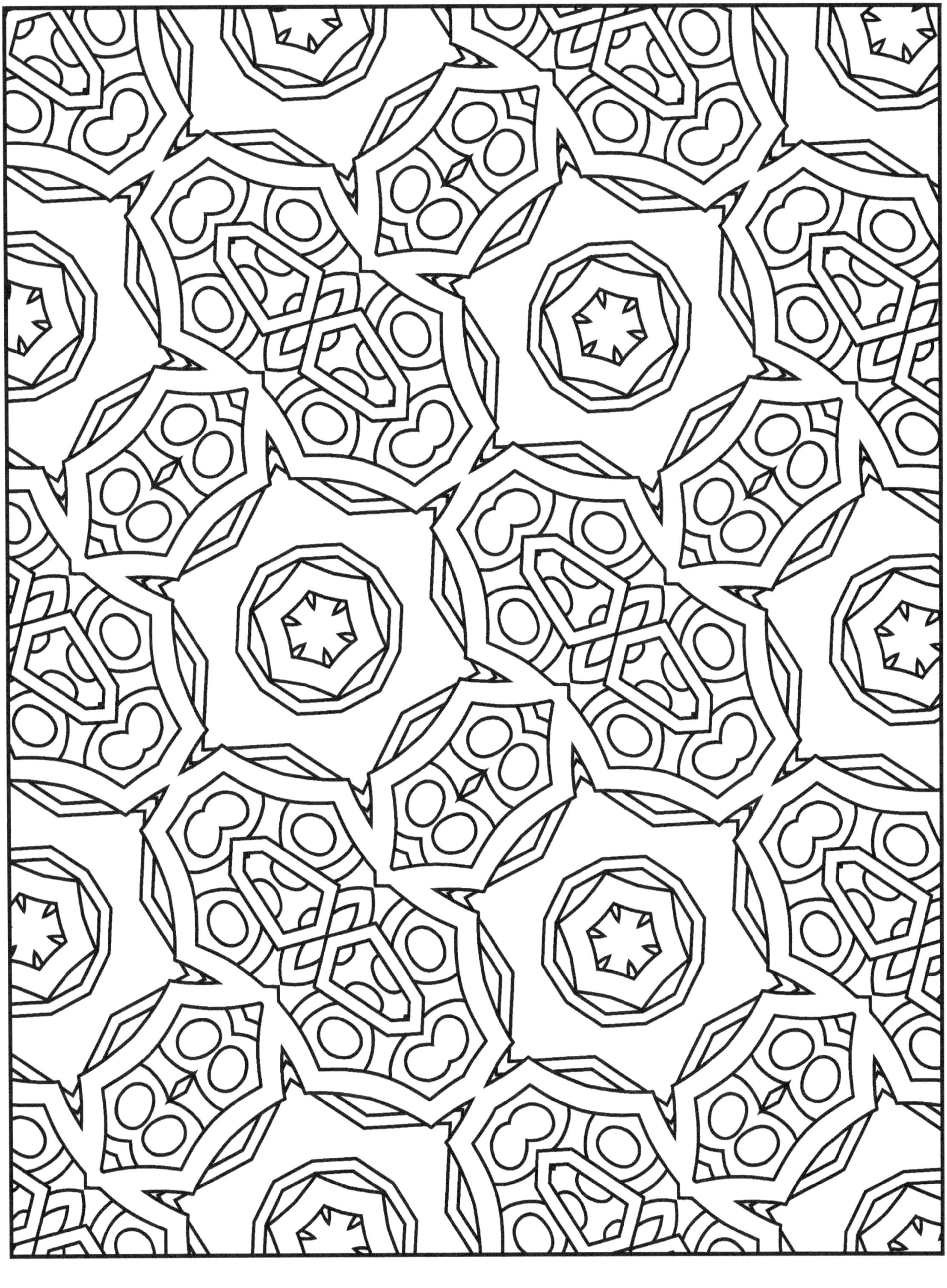

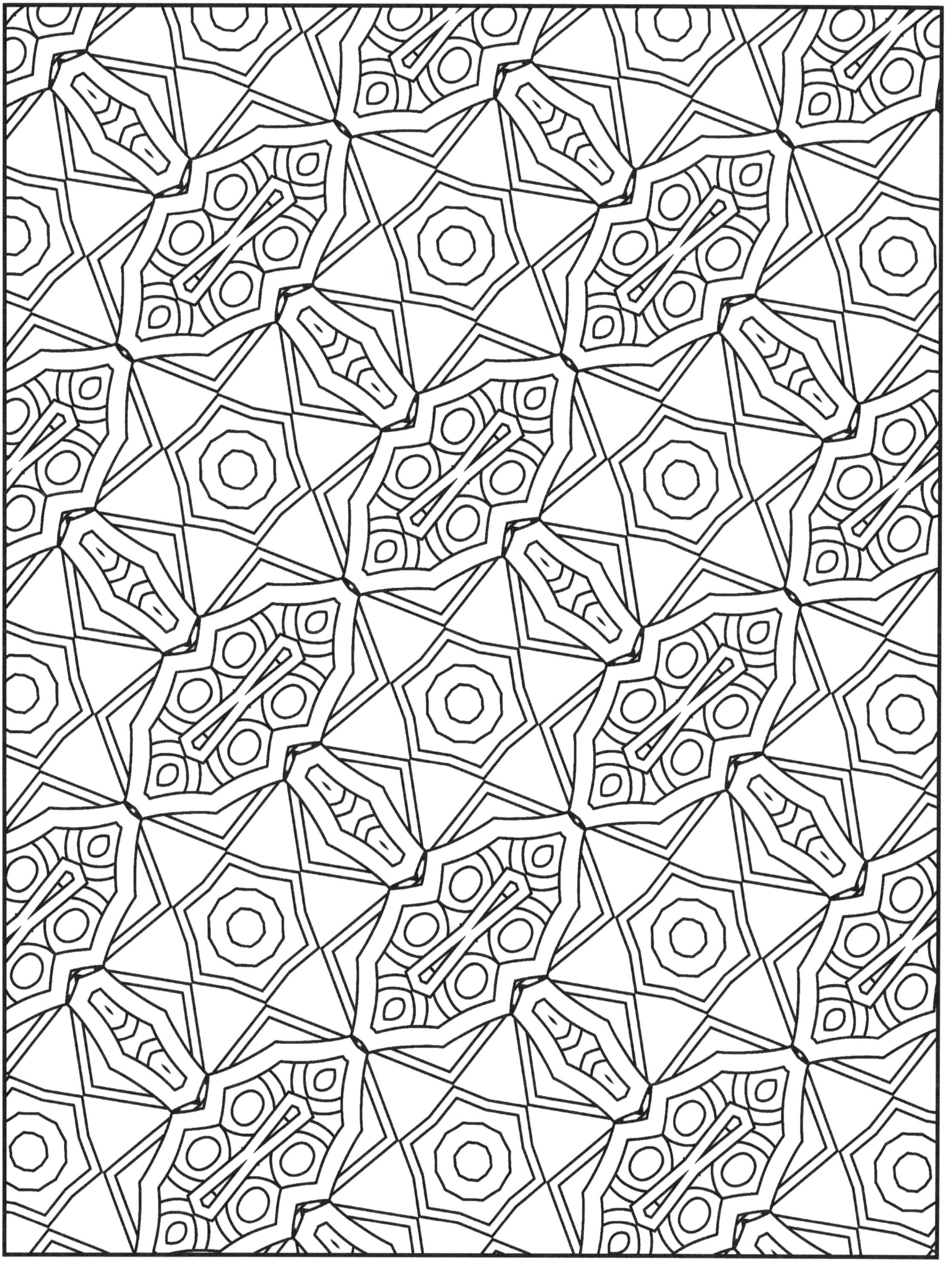

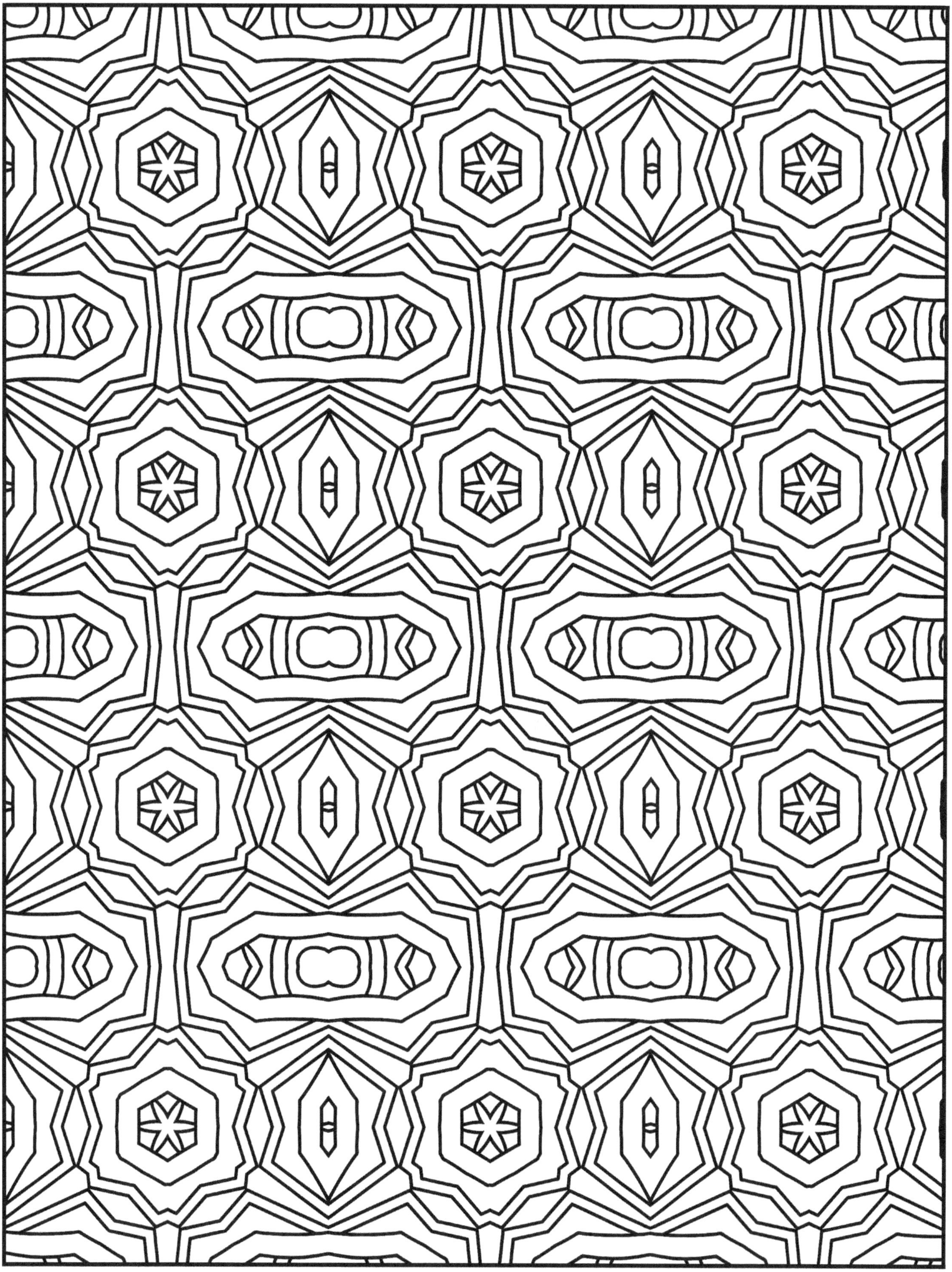

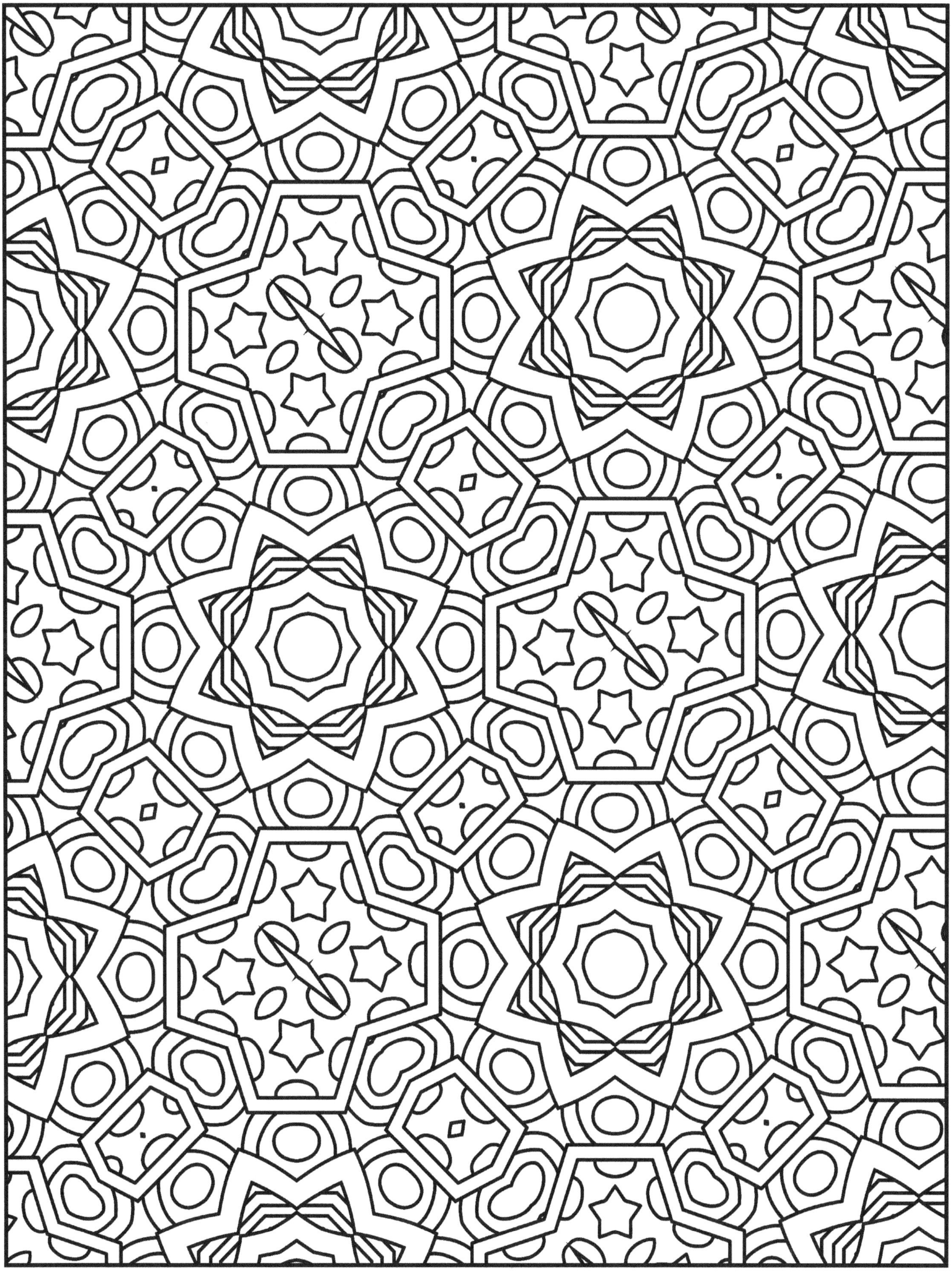

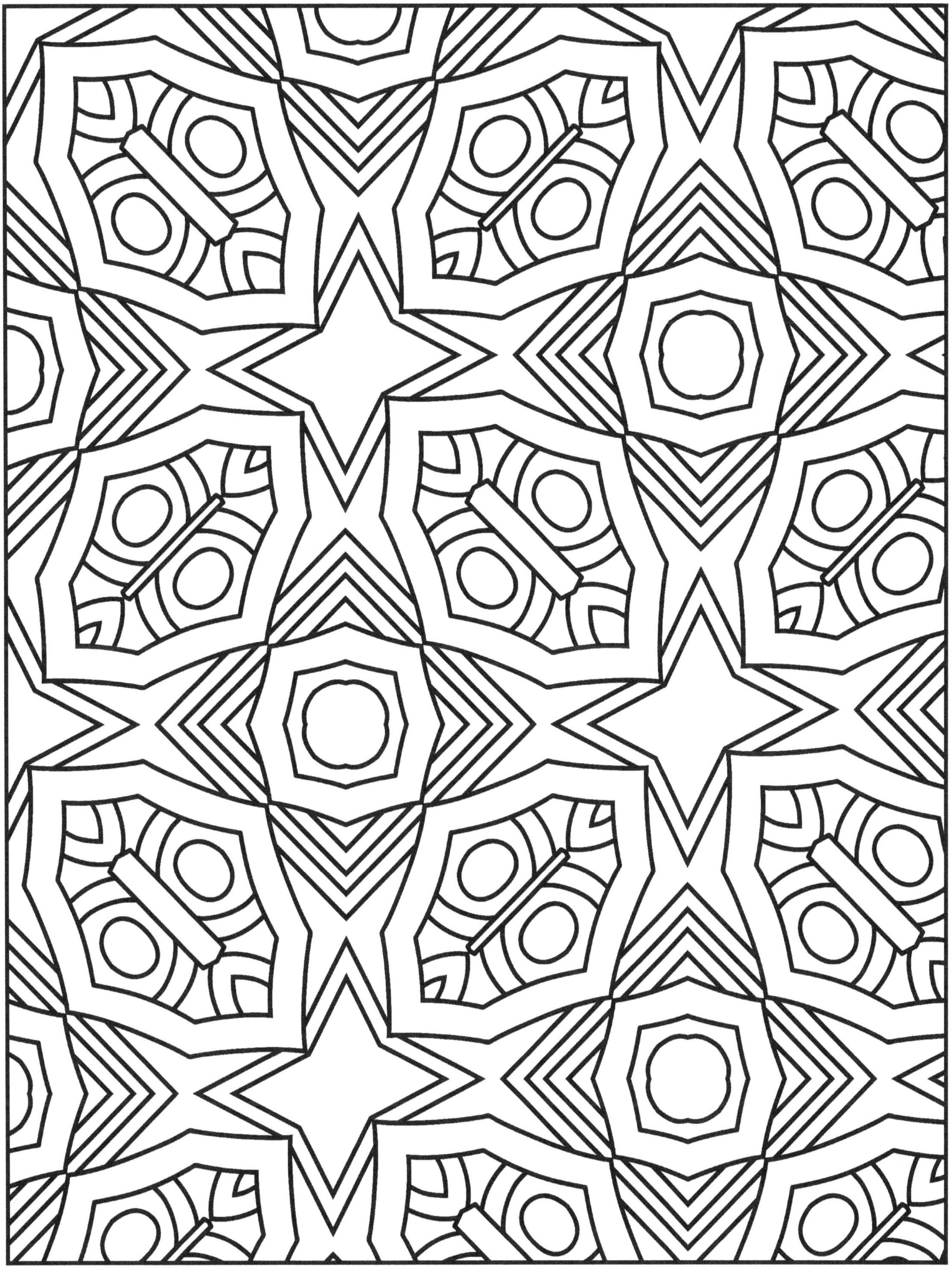

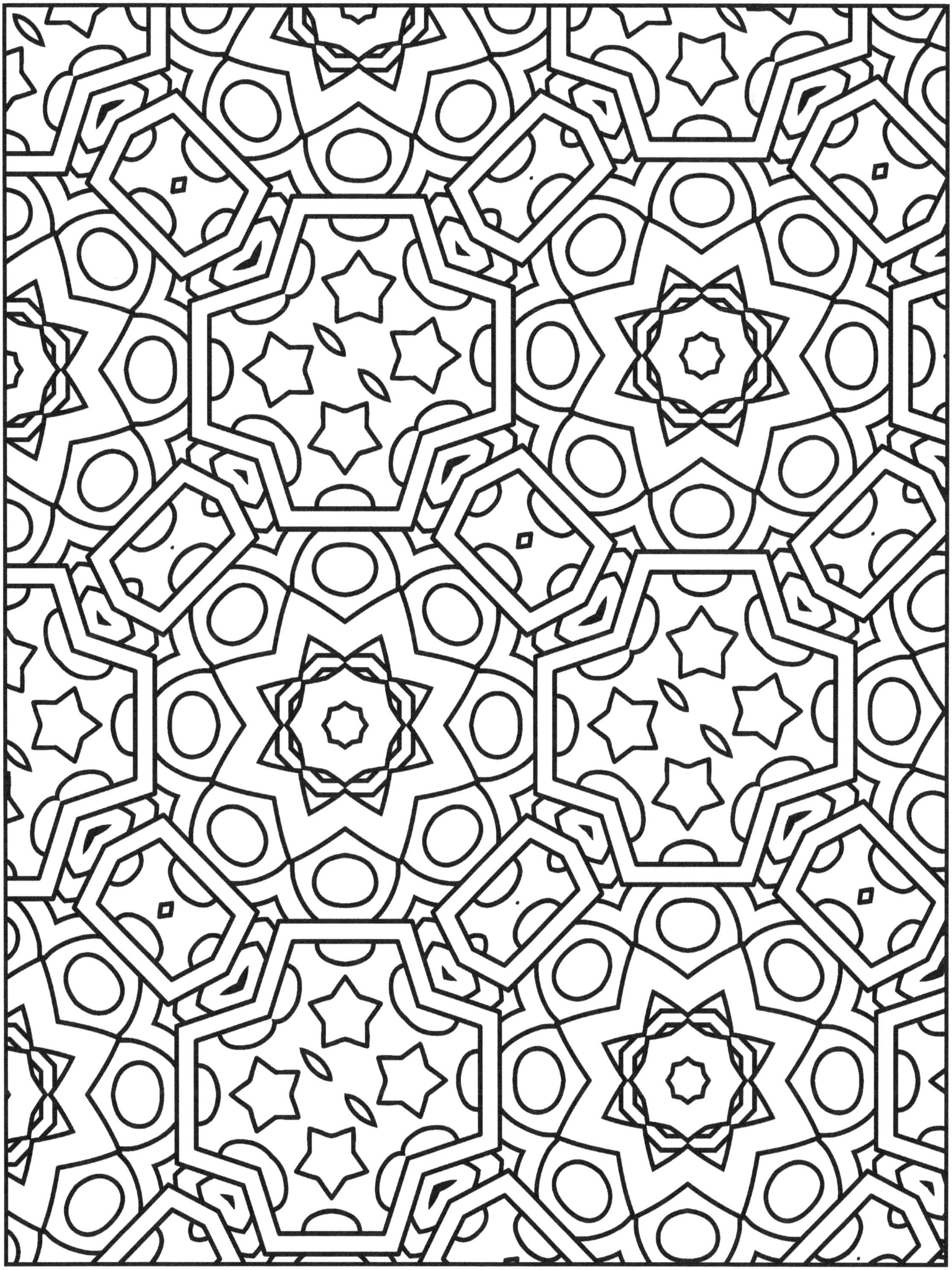

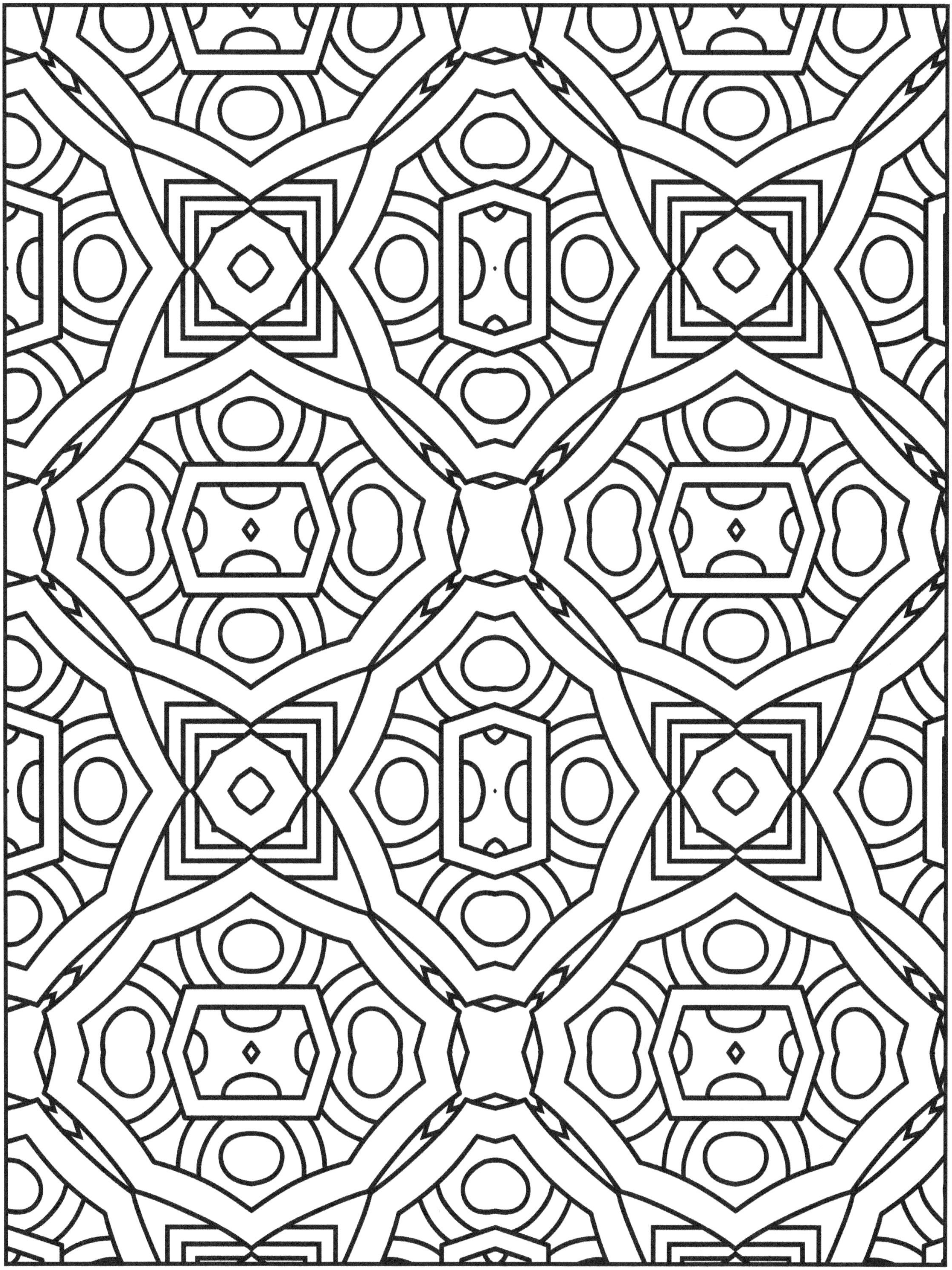

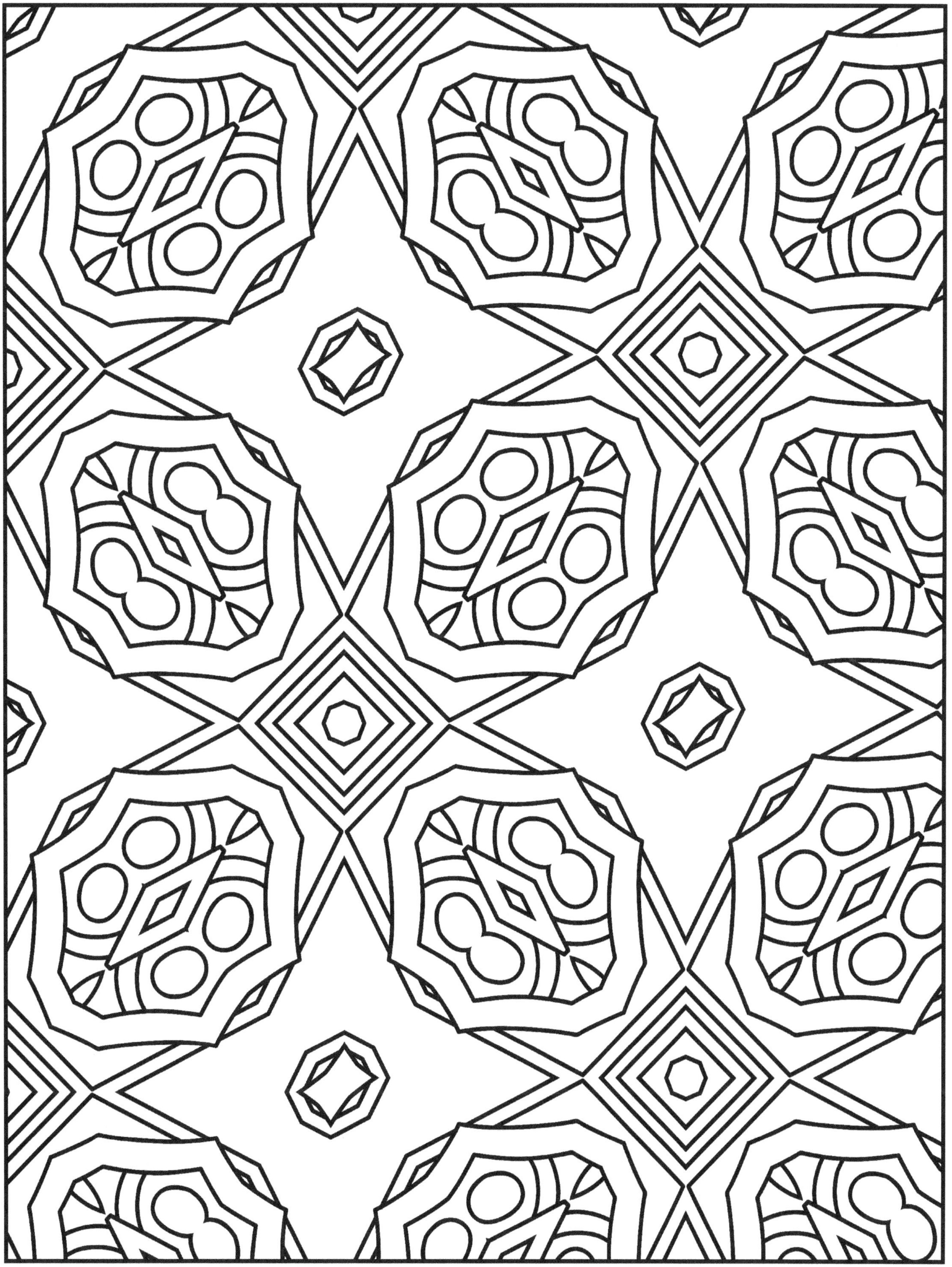

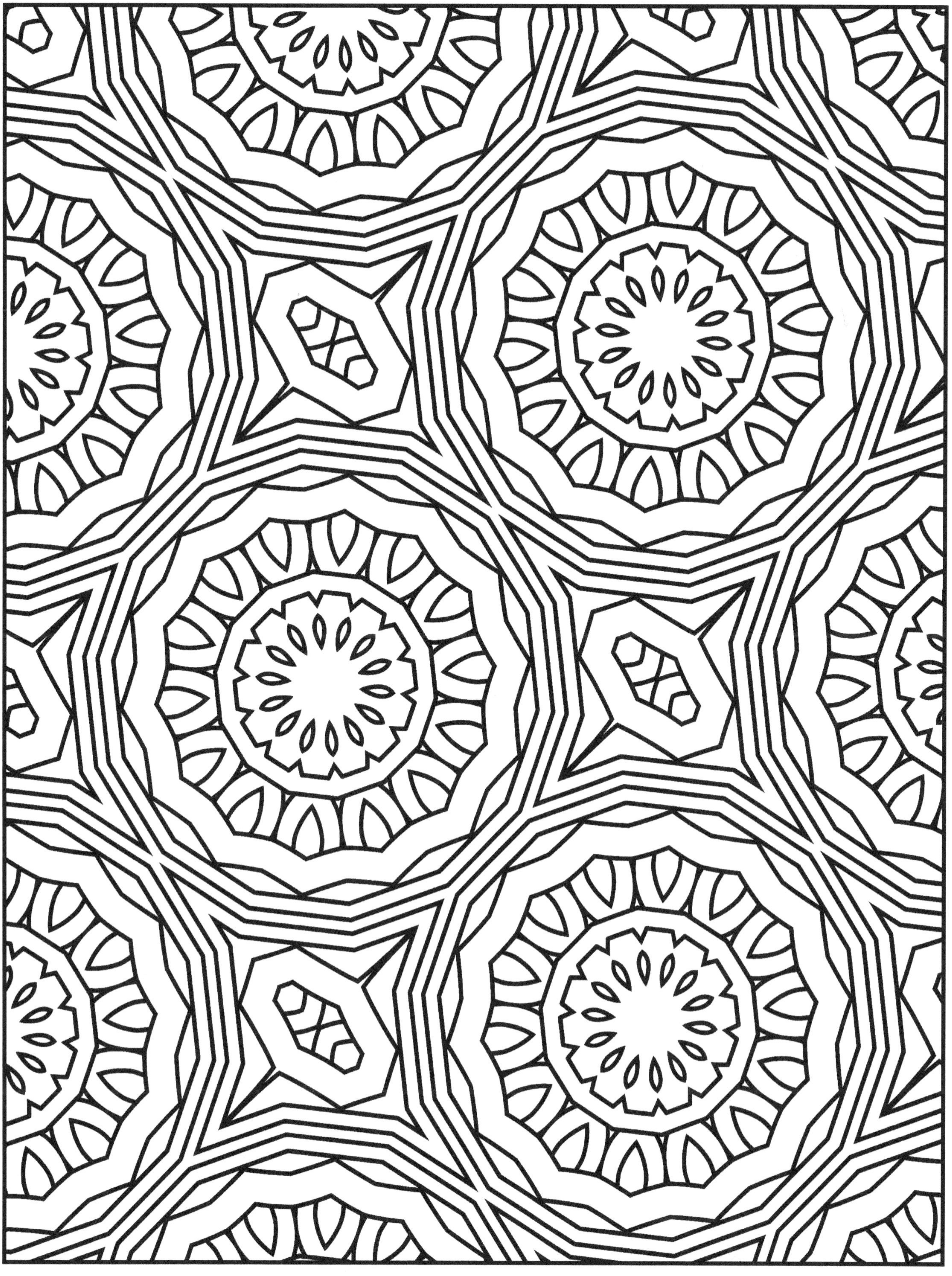

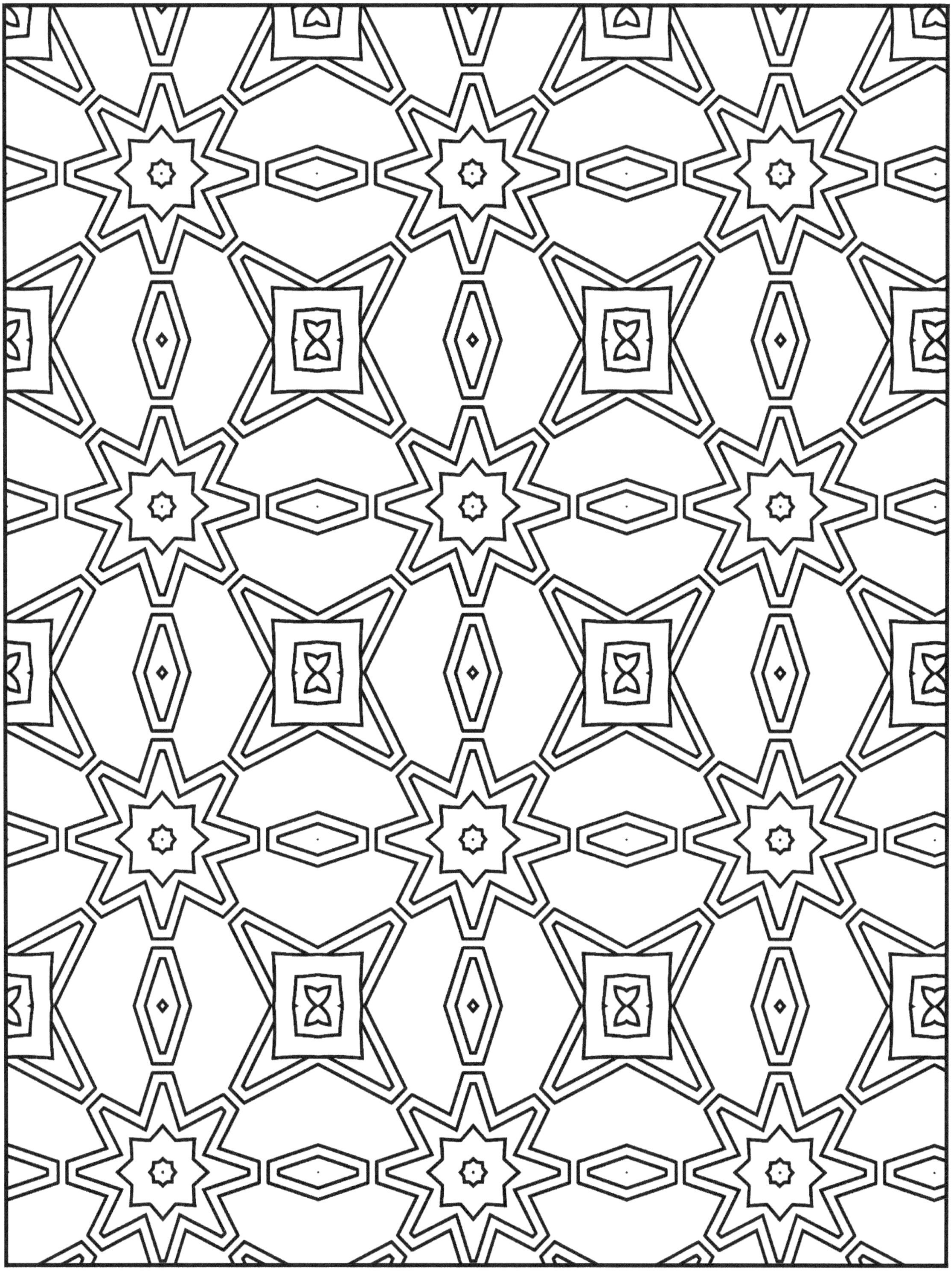

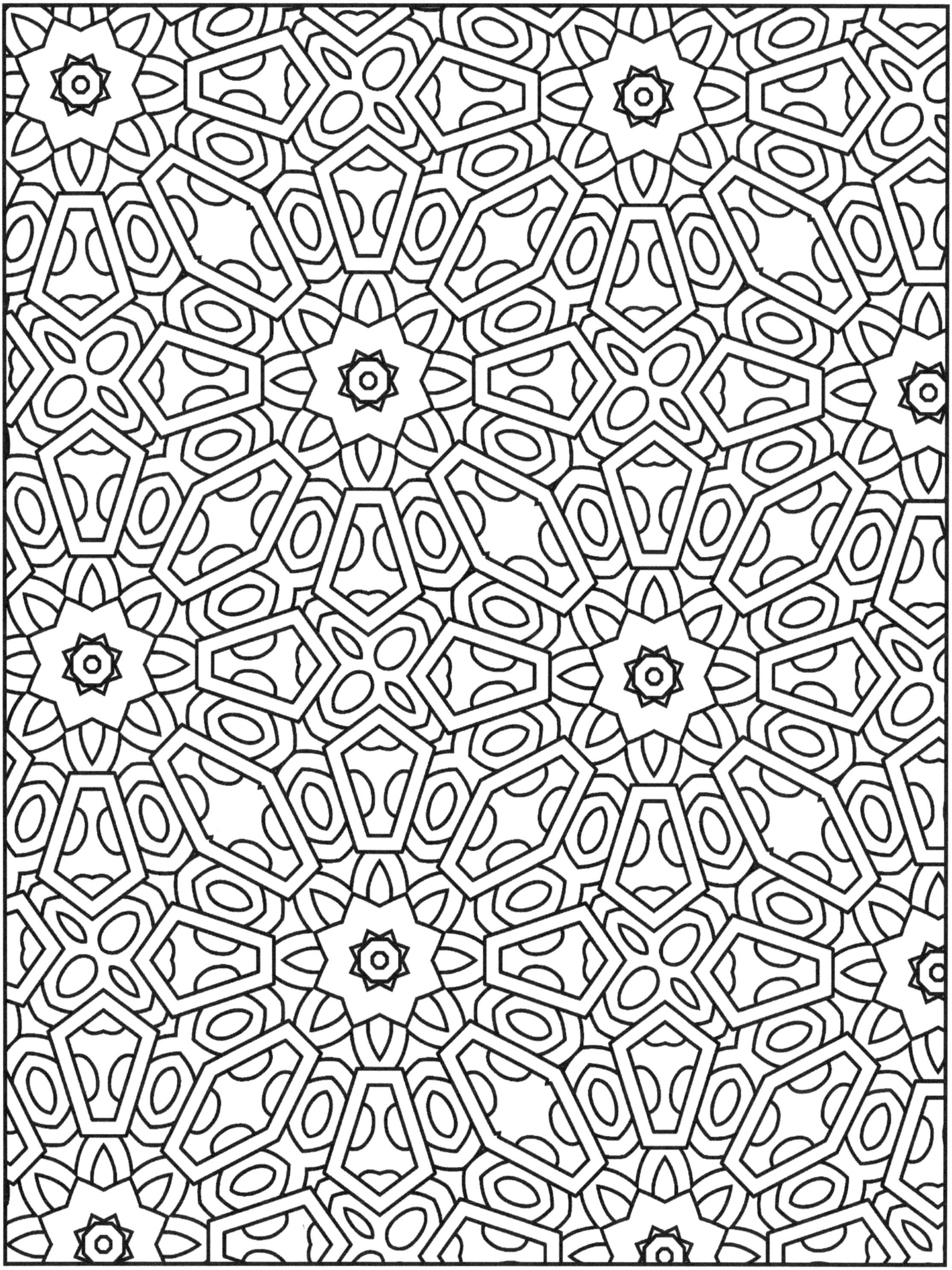

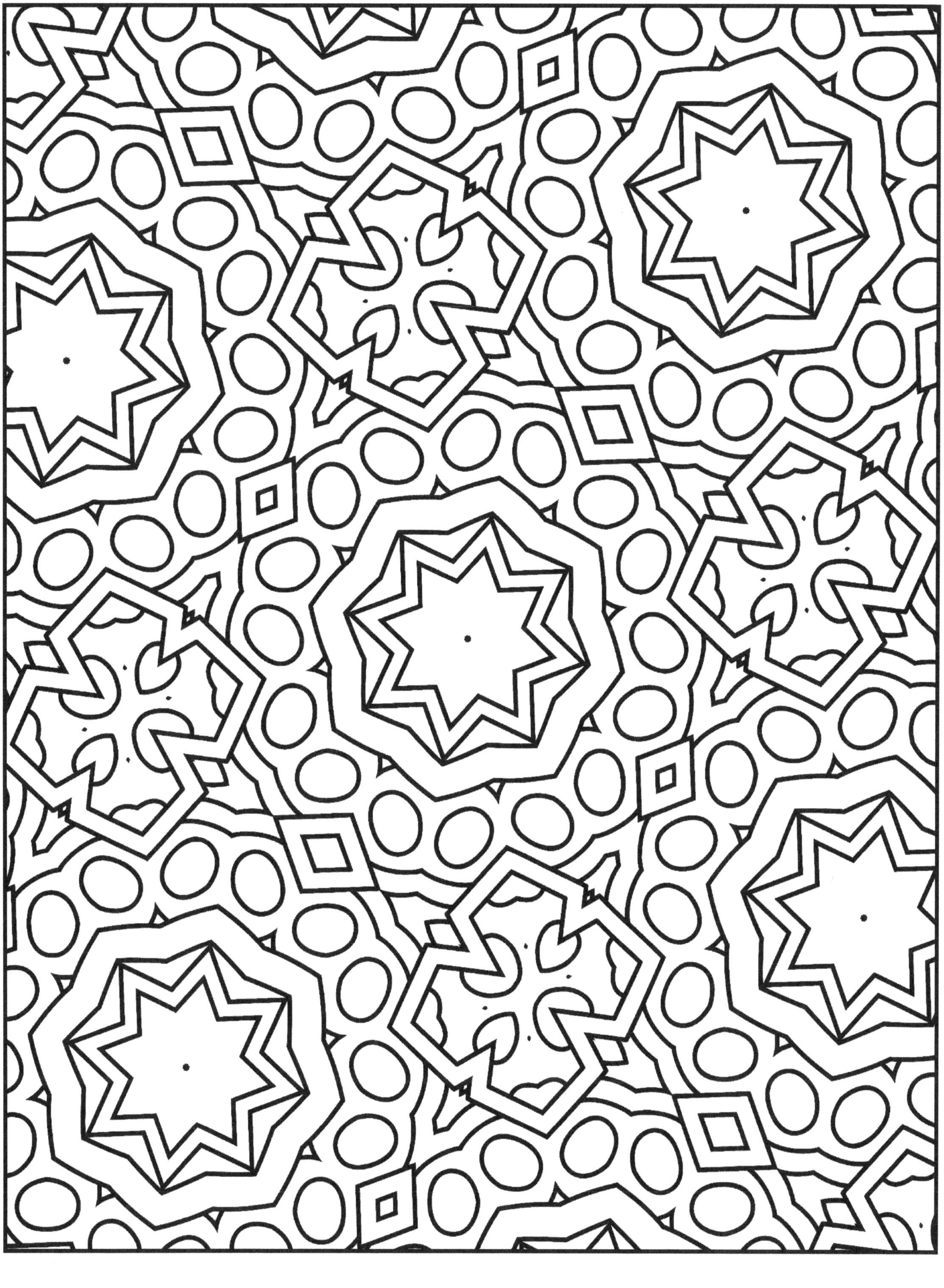

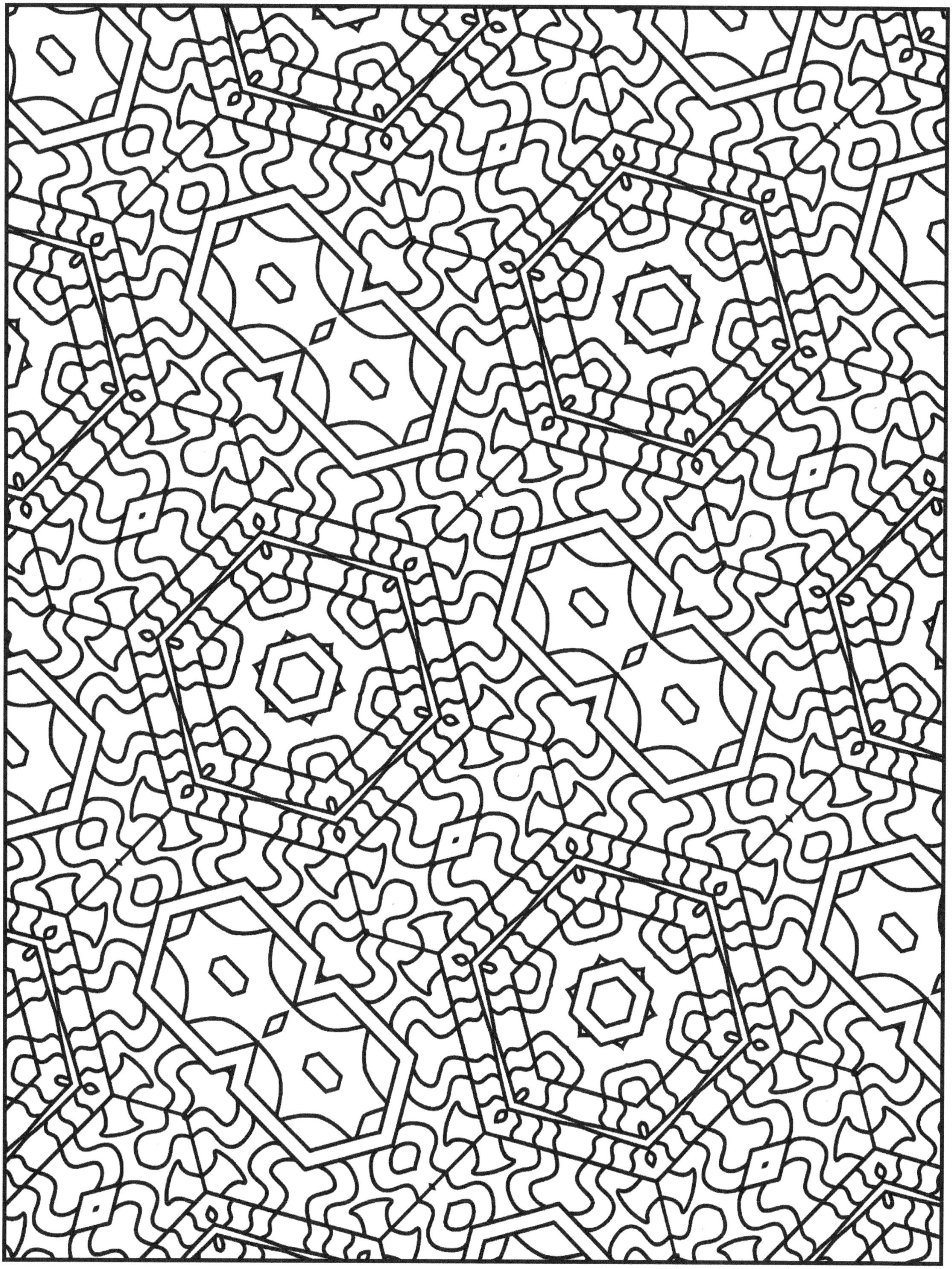

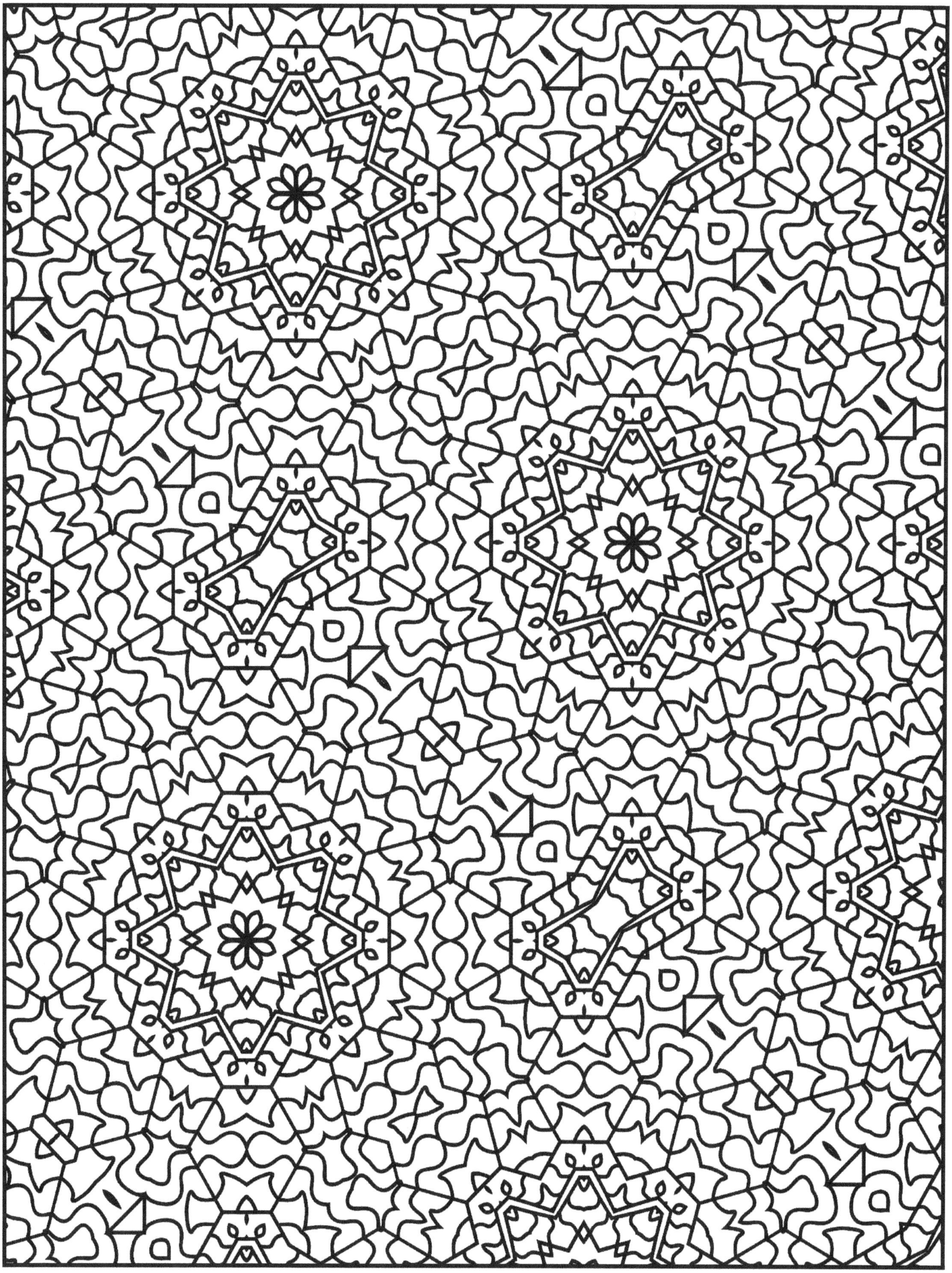

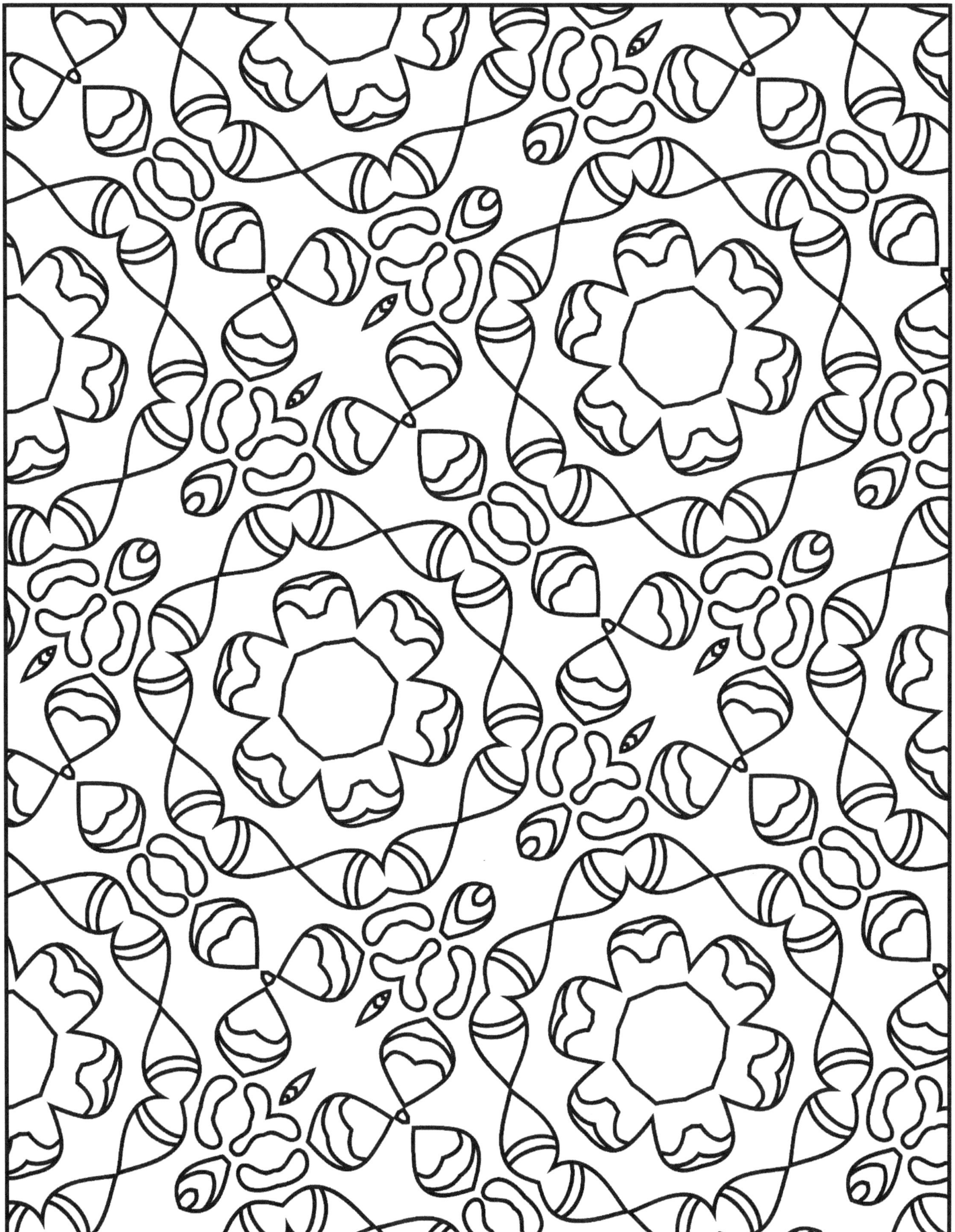

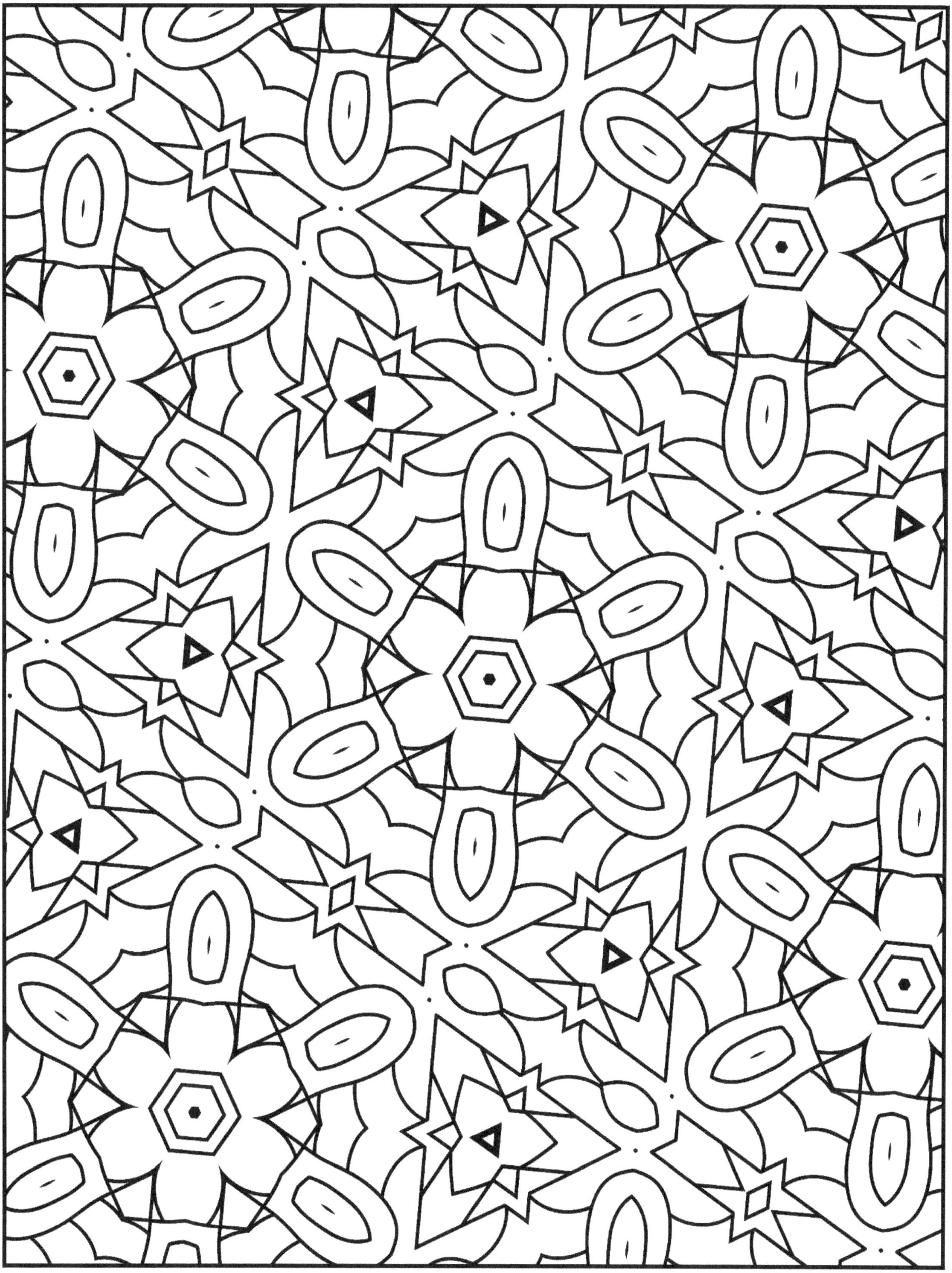

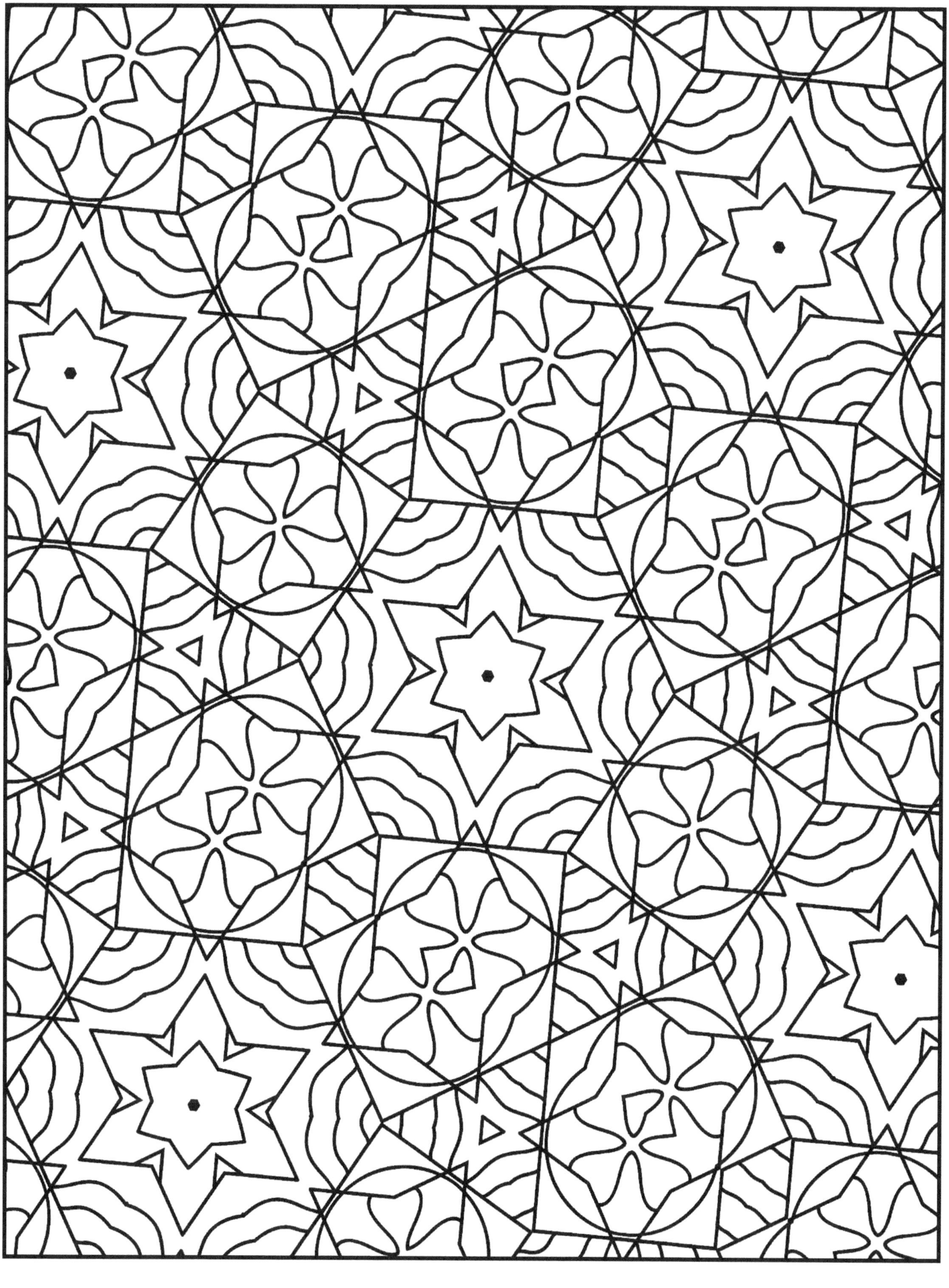

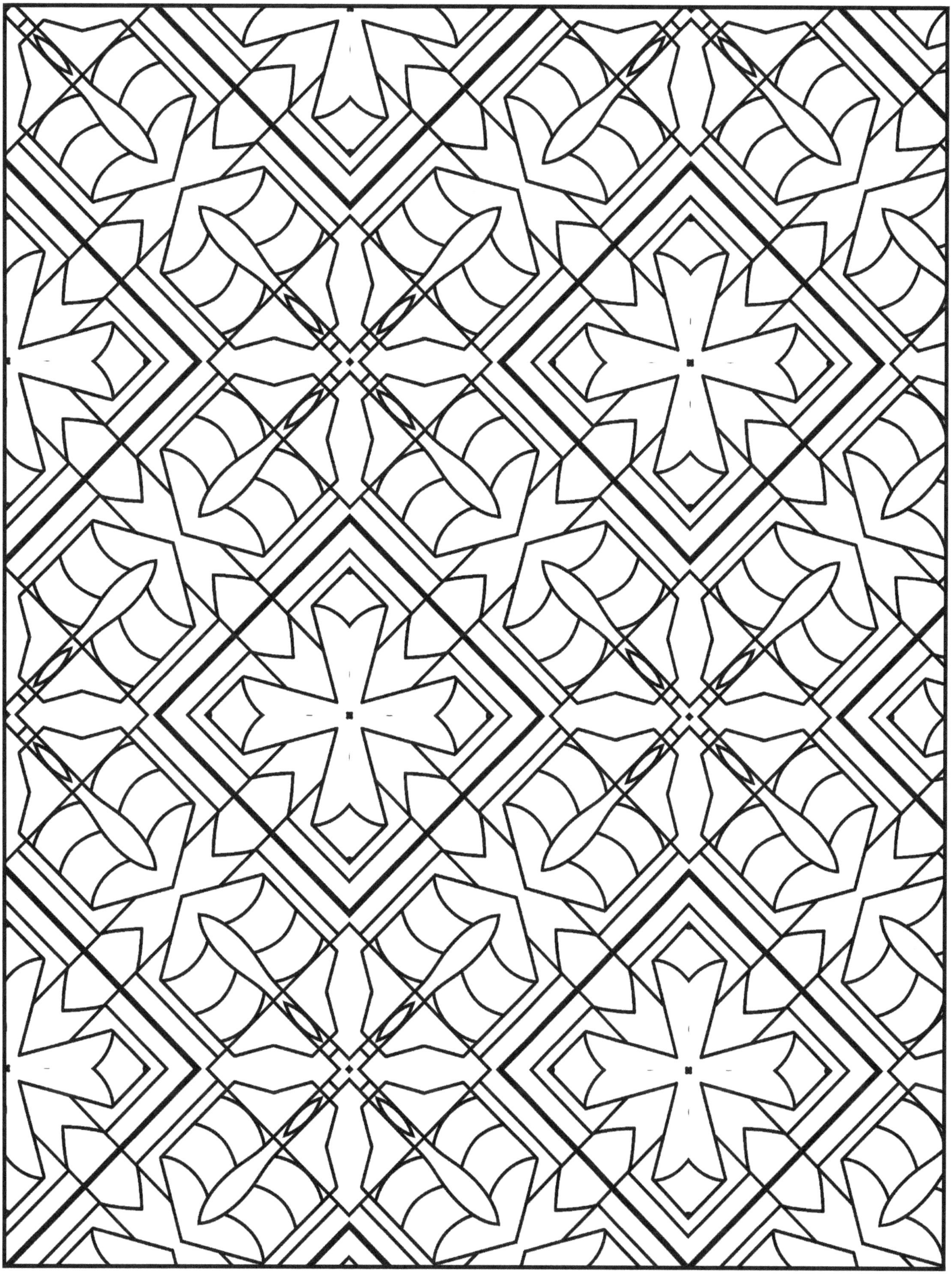

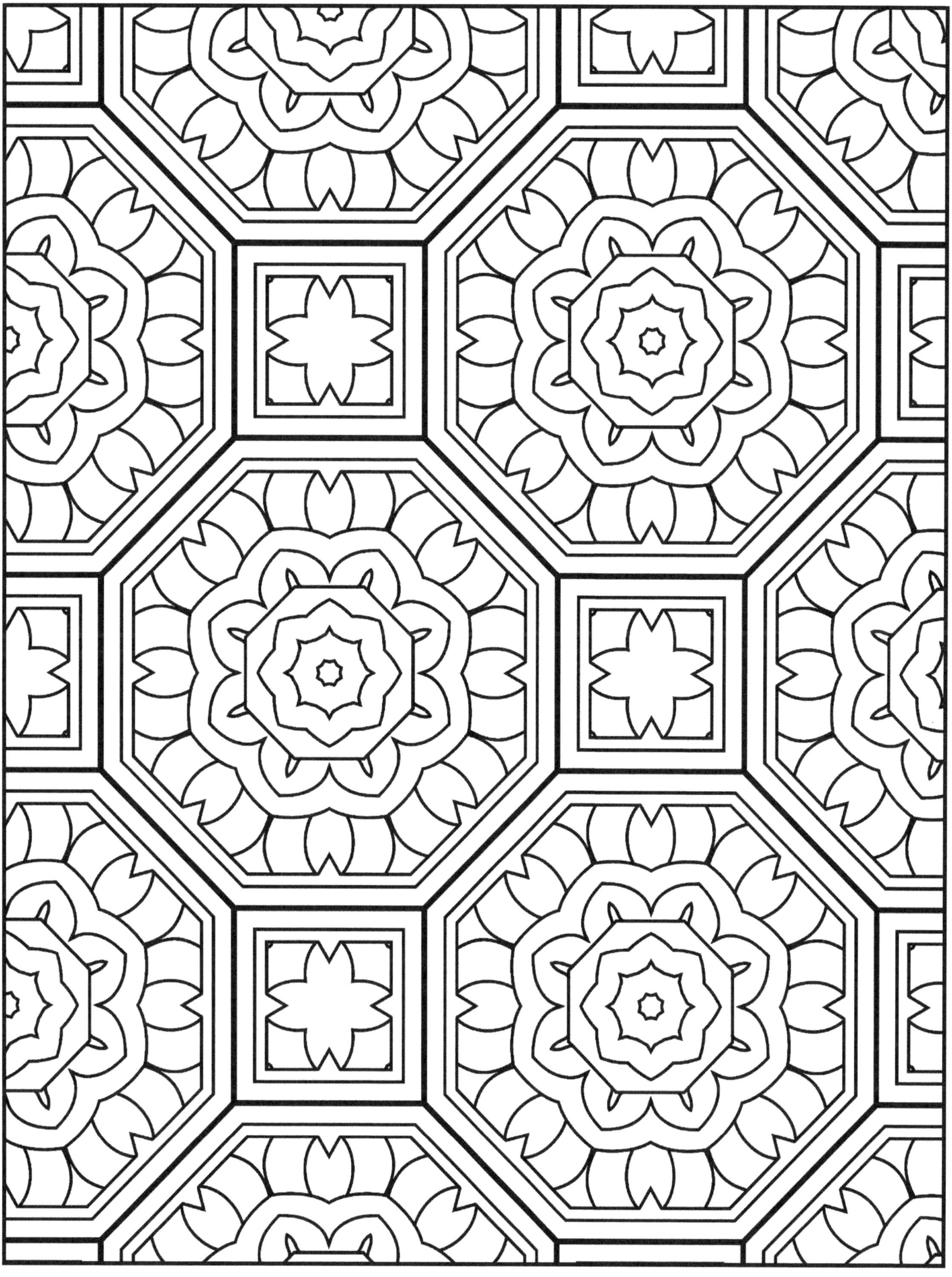

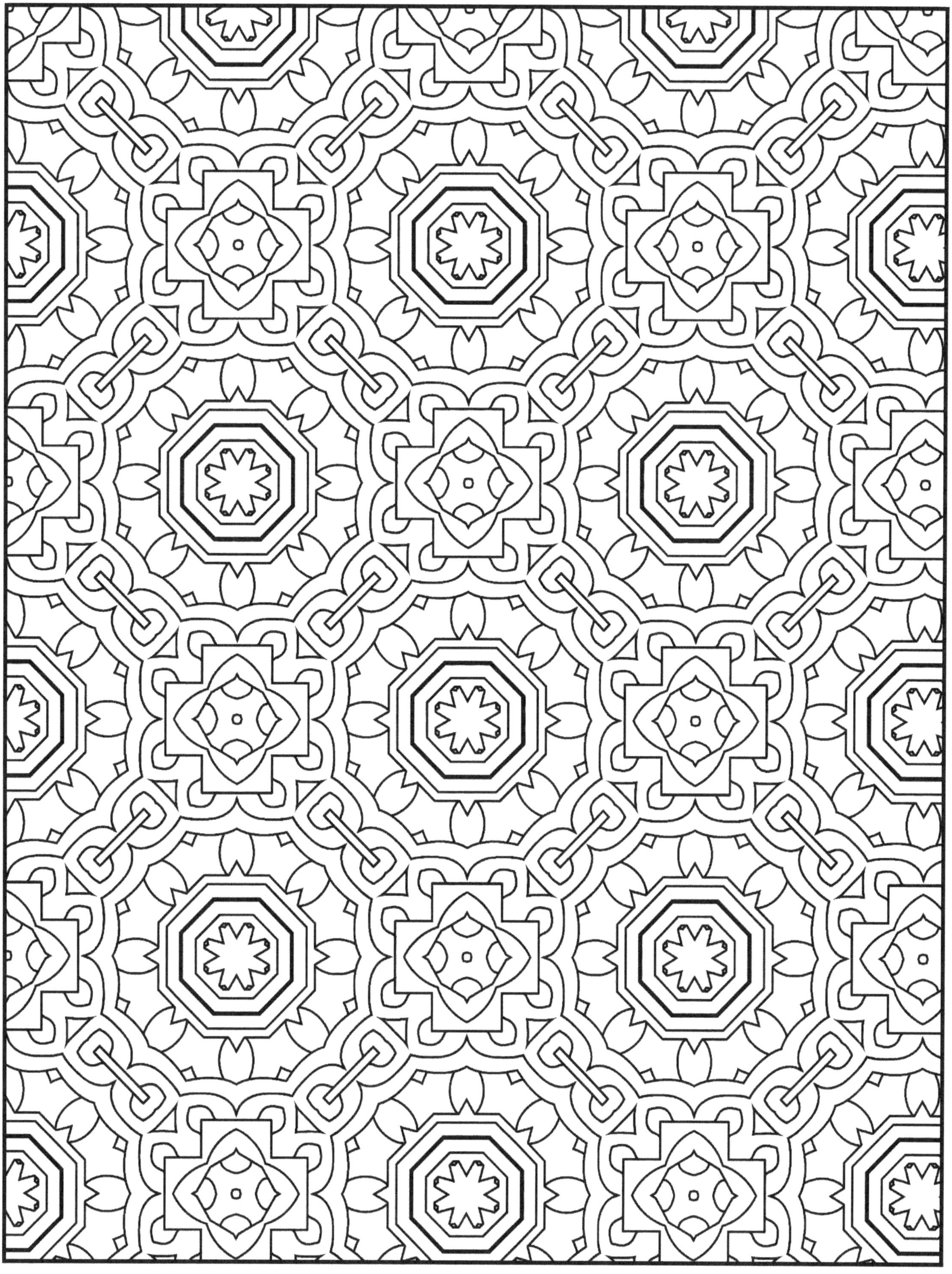

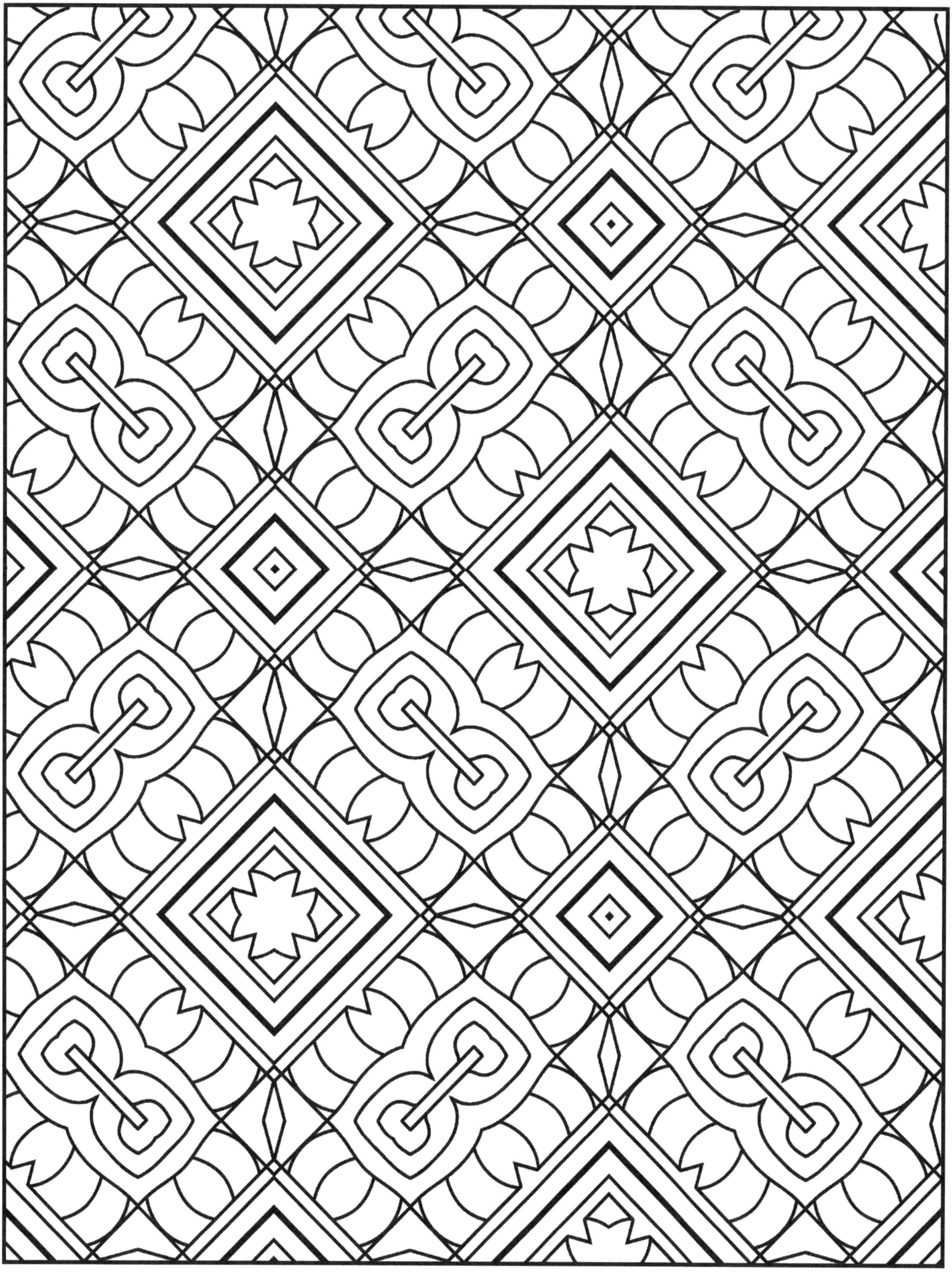

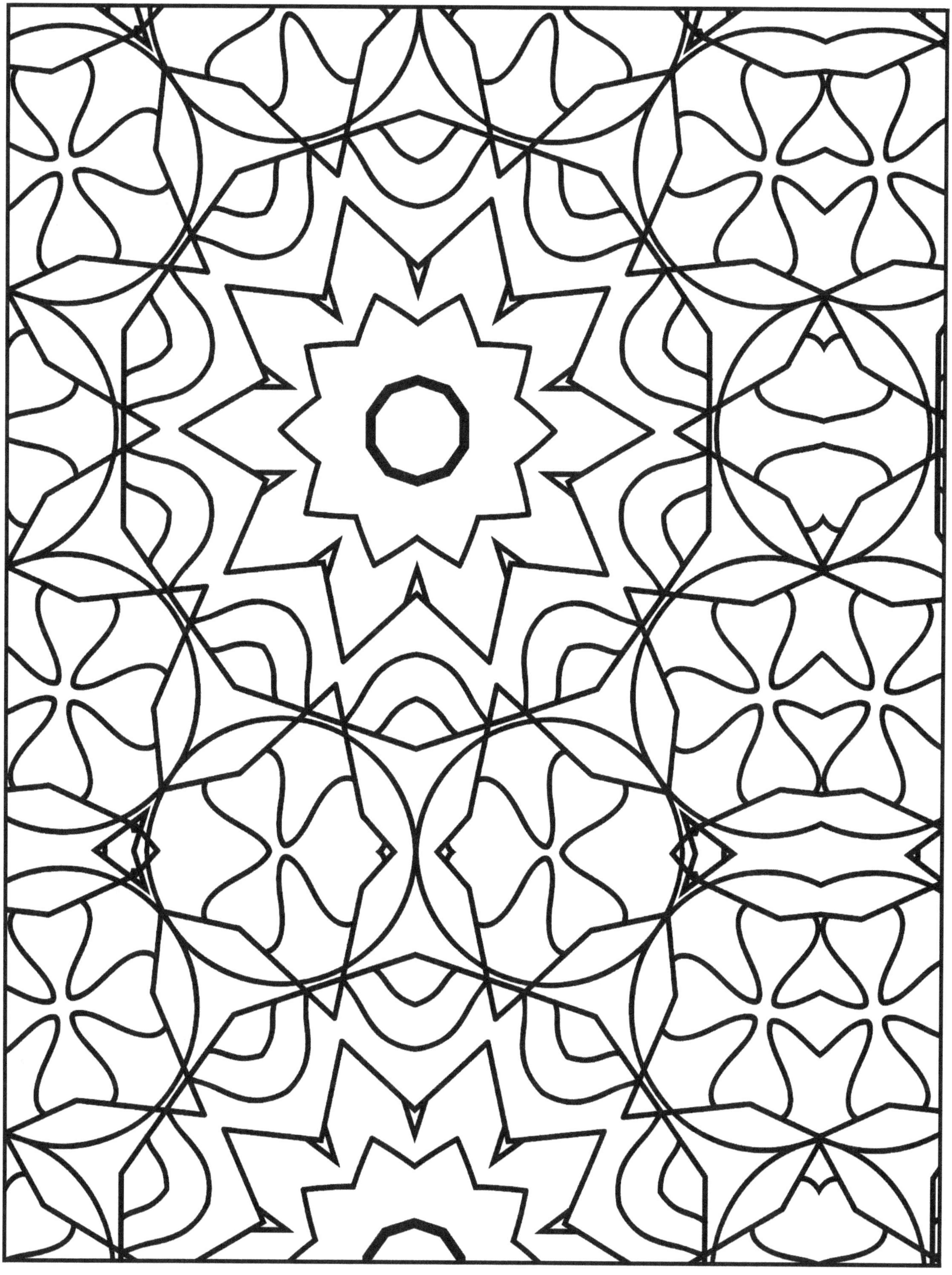

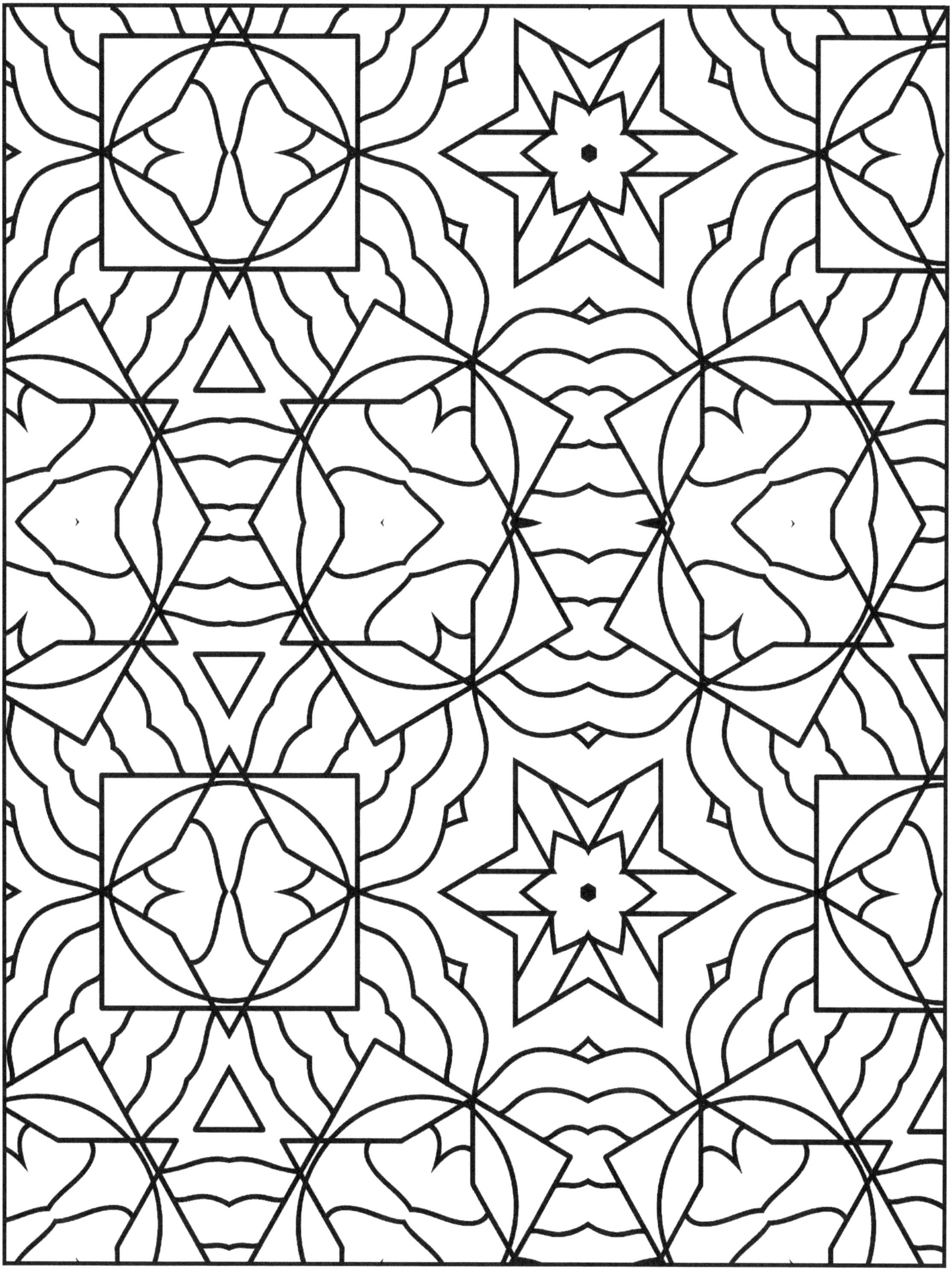

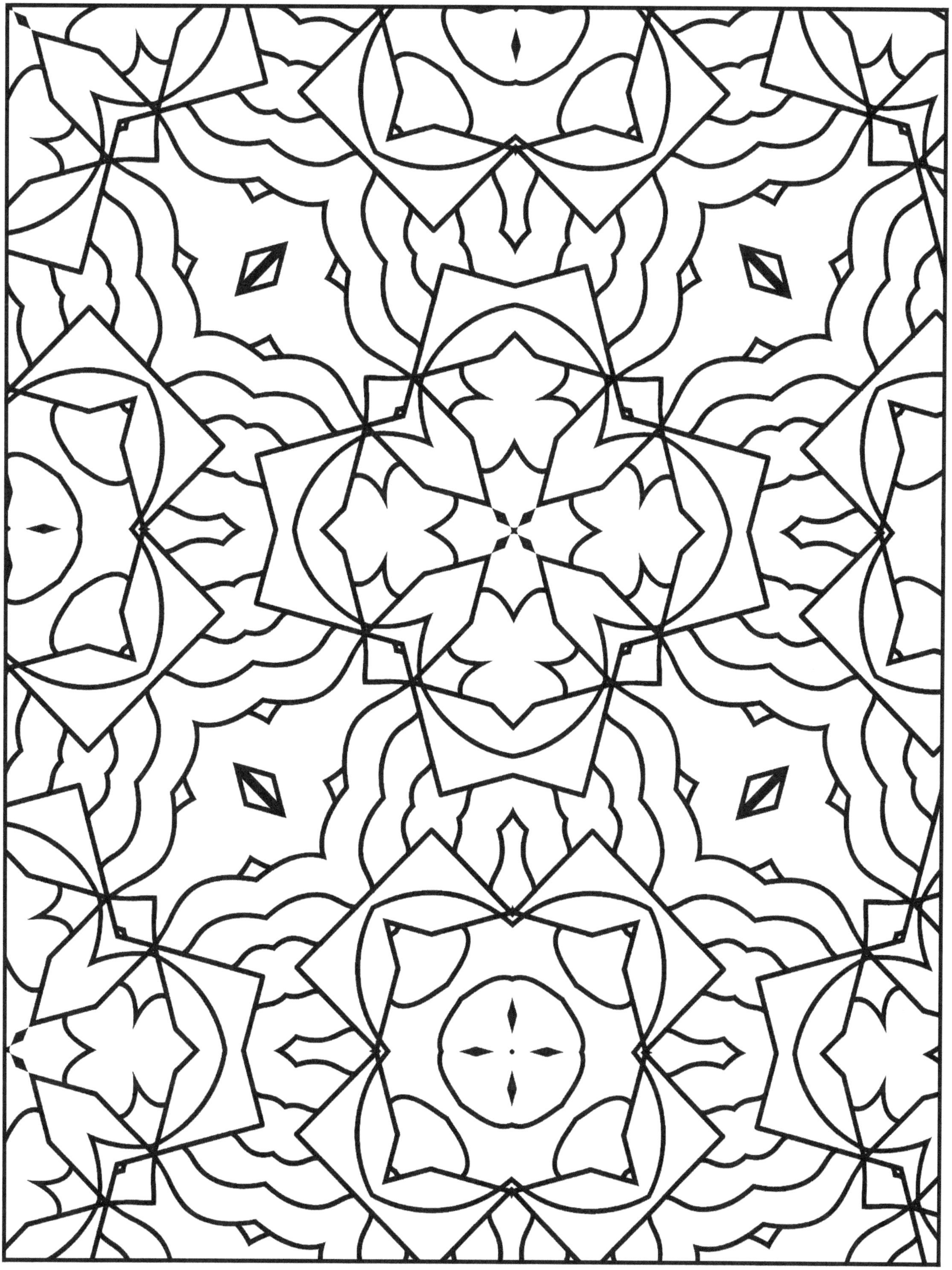

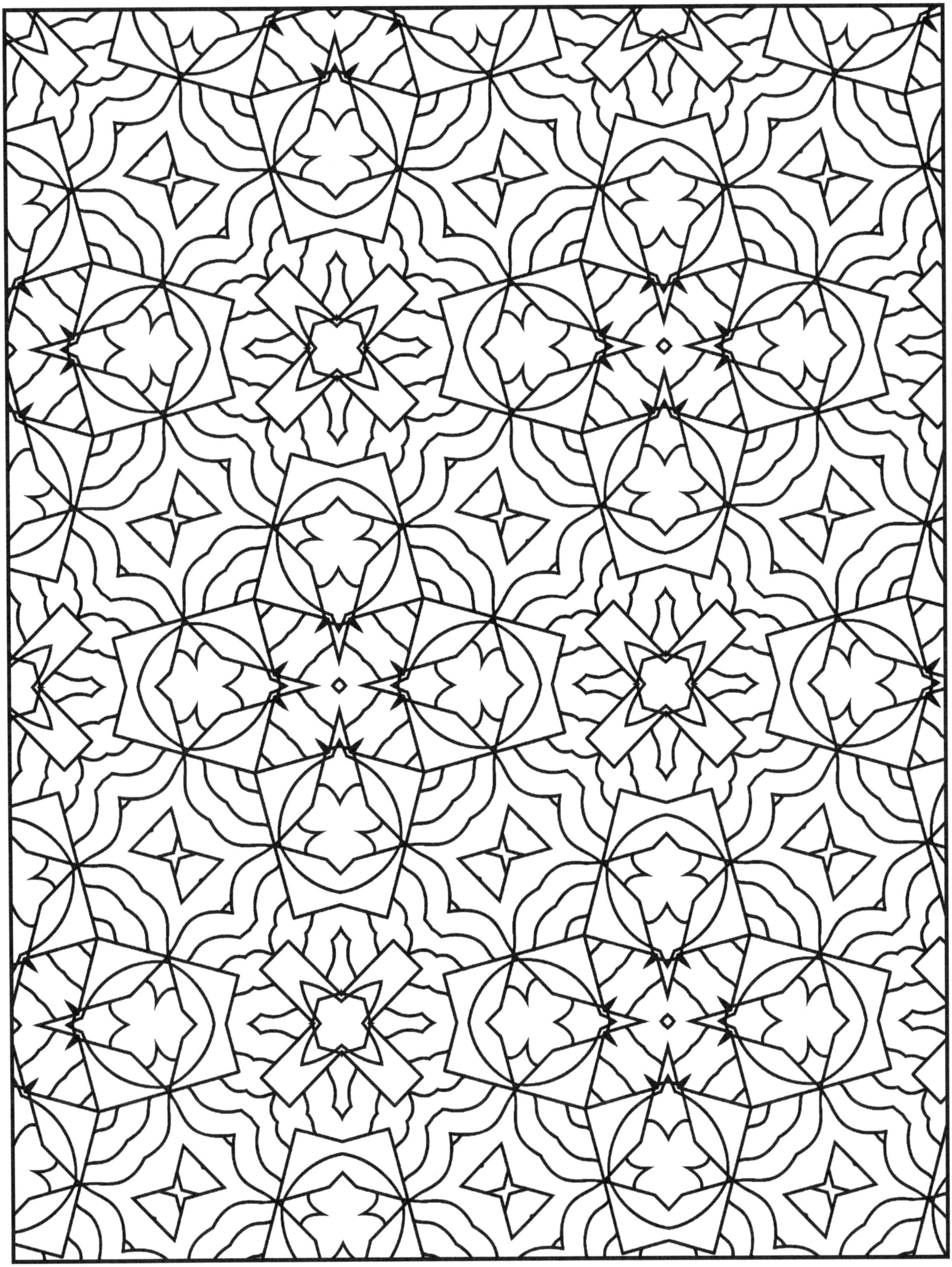

www.ingramcontent.com/pod-product-compliance
Lightning Source LLC
Chambersburg PA
CBHW081118180526
45170CB00008B/2897
9781541337312